SUCCESS IN SUCCESSION

Success in Succession
Heaven's Blueprints for Transition in Life and Leadership

Copyright © 2023 Terry Moore and Chris McRae

All rights reserved. No part of this publication may be reproduced in a retrieval system, or transmitted in any form or by any means—electronic, mechanical, photocopying, recording, or otherwise—without the prior written permission of the publisher.

Unless otherwise noted, scripture taken from the New King James Version®. Copyright © 1982 by Thomas Nelson. Used by permission. All rights reserved. | Scripture references marked (NIV) taken from the Holy Bible, New International Version®, NIV®. Copyright © 1973, 1978, 1984, 2011 by Biblica, Inc.™ Used by permission of Zondervan. All rights reserved worldwide. www.zondervan.com The "NIV" and "New International Version" are trademarks registered in the United States Patent and Trademark Office by Biblica, Inc.™ | Scripture quotations marked (PARA) are paraphrased versions of the original passage by the author, while maintaining fidelity to the original Hebrew, Greek, and Aramaic texts.

This manuscript has undergone viable editorial work and proofreading, yet human limitations may have resulted in minor grammatical or syntax-related errors remaining in the finished book. The understanding of the reader is requested in these cases. While precaution has been taken in the preparation of this book, the publisher and author assume no responsibility for errors or omissions, or for damages resulting from the use of the information contained herein.

This book is set in the typeface *Athelas* designed by Veronika Burian and Jose Scaglione.

Paperback ISBN: 978-1-955546-50-8
Hardcover ISBN: 979-8-8689-9765-5

A Publication of *Tall Pine Books*
119 E Center Street, Suite B4A | Warsaw, Indiana 46580
www.tallpinebooks.com

| 1 23 23 20 16 02 |

Published in the United States of America

SUCCESS IN SUCCESSION

HEAVEN'S BLUEPRINTS FOR TRANSITION IN LIFE AND LEADERSHIP

TERRY MOORE AND CHRIS MCRAE

FOREWORD

TERRY MOORE AND his wife, Susan, attended a Bible conference I hosted in San Antonio, Texas, in 1982. The Holy Spirit moved on the entire group in a powerful way. Terry and Susan, along with some of their closest friends, were totally transformed by the power of the Holy Spirit. They actually experienced what it means to "lose your life seeking to fulfill God's kingdom purpose" in the here and now. They realized God did not leave us here to get us out of here, but to reveal Jesus to the world He gave His life to redeem.

With a fresh zeal for the Lord, Terry began to lead a home group Bible study, with Susan by his side. Not surprisingly, it exploded. Within a few years, the gathering had outgrown their home, and Terry sensed God was calling him to step aside from his business ventures and go into full-time ministry. He founded Sojourn Church in 1987.

Terry has successfully led the church to make a kingdom impact in obedience to Christ's commission. He has inspired amazing growth in many pastors, local church members and business leaders. In addition, he serves on the Board of Trustees for LIFE Outreach International.

I've had the privilege of speaking at Sojourn Church over the years and know firsthand that Terry has discipled his flock well. He is humble, an exceptional teacher and leads as a servant.

Chris McRae, who began serving at Sojourn in 1996, is an evangelist at heart, and his gifts complement Terry's. In October 2021, almost two years after Terry passed the baton to Chris, I was invited to speak at Sojourn. Chris has never met a stranger and welcomed me with open arms. The emphasis was "Harvest of Souls," and I gave a clear gospel message with an altar call. I sweated so much that Chris gave me an extra shirt he had in his office to wear home and keep.

When Terry moved out of his senior role in January 2020, he didn't move to Palm Springs to play golf every day or simply retire on a ranch. In fact, he notes that *retirement* is never mentioned in the Bible. "Our purpose continues until the day we leave the planet, and retirement is just not something I really ever consider," he says. "It is not an excuse to be idle or unfruitful in the kingdom."

In his role as founding pastor, Terry oversees the missions and financial aspect of Sojourn. He also continues to co-teach with Chris on Wednesday nights. Chris has learned the value of strategy. "Pastor Terry is a strategic thinker, and one of the reasons the church was so successful was because he was always thinking at least a year in advance," he says. Chris has been deeply impacted by the supernatural influence of Terry.

In his new role, Chris embraces Terry's feedback, correction, insight and foresight. "Not once have I felt he was meddling or attempting to pull levers behind the scenes," he says.

The transition at Sojourn has been smooth, thanks to wise planning and two yielded hearts who are committed to kingdom work. In this book, they share practical steps that will help other pastors and leaders, including questions to ask when choosing the next leader, business matters that involve bylaws and a well-written transition plan for key personnel.

The insights presented will help other successfully navigate these waters and position a church or organization for continued growth. As Terry shares, "We would all do well to position ourselves the way Paul did, that is, to be able to say with confidence, 'I have fought the good fight, I have finished the race, I have kept the faith. Now there is in store for me the crown of righteousness, which the Lord, the righteous Judge, will award to me on that day...'" (2 Timothy 4:7-8).

—JAMES ROBISON
Founder and President, *LIFE Outreach International*
Fort Worth, Texas

CONTENTS

Introduction 1

1. The Approach 5
2. The Inheritance 27
3. The Storms 47
4. The Myths 63
5. The Plan 79
6. The Family 105
7. The Adjustment 123
8. The Aftermath 141

Afterword 153
Endnotes 155
About the Authors 157

INTRODUCTION

Co-Authored

CONTRARY TO POPULAR belief, it is possible to *enjoy* transition and not merely *endure* it. Our goal in putting this book together is to provide insights that maximize your God-ordained shift. Many of these principles have been hard-earned through our own experiences in the ever-changing world of ministry. Change can be scary to navigate, and if you don't follow a biblical blueprint, you will want to transition *out* of your transition before it's even finished.

While the book will be relevant for all types of transitions, the thread that we will pull throughout these pages is our own story of seeing God's succession plan play out within Sojourn Church. The truth is, independent congregations all over America are in states of crisis as pastors age and local bodies are being entrusted to new leaders. A recent Barna study found that only 22% of Christians who had recently experienced a leadership transition found it to be a *positive* experience. Another 71% either saw the transition as negative or some mixture of good and bad. That same study found that during these transitions, the strongest negative emotion for the incoming pastor, outgoing pastor, and the congregation alike was one thing: *worry*.[1]

Through a combination of Spirit-led decisions and wise planning, you can quell fears and establish the peace of God right in the midst of your big change. This book aims to provide a framework for approaching transition, tools to keep in mind during the process, and insight in charting a new course *after* the shift. We will talk through the practical side of succession planning, work through rich biblical accounts, and bust common myths on the subject.

In writing this book, we certainly don't want to convey to the reader that we did everything perfectly. There are *always* areas with room for improvement in any human undertaking. If we are honest with ourselves, we can easily look back and find shortcomings. At the same time, we can look back and see what *worked*. Our hope is that this book provides both a path to success and a caution against the pitfalls of major change.

Our goal in putting this together was to keep the

book relevant to organizations and individuals. Yes, we want pastors who are transitioning churches to glean from the content. At the same time, we want the student going off to college to pull from the insight, as well. From taking a church to taking a road trip, the universal truths here should apply to anyone gearing up for change. These truths have never been more relevant as people are changing jobs more often, remote work has folks moving more freely, and culture is undergoing major change seemingly every week.

Transition is an inevitable part of life. We all expect change to happen. However, the timing and circumstances of that change are often *unexpected*. In the same way that no two humans are the same, no two transitions are the same. Everyone is different, which means change is not a perfect science. At the same time, there is a perfect God with flawless principles to give us, and following His orders would serve us all very well on our journey.

Whether you are passing the reins, getting the reins, or just observing a transition, we hope you find something of value in these pages. During times of upheaval when it feels that everything is changing all the time, we have the comfort of a God who changes not. Let's lean into His heart and better our world in the process.

CHAPTER ONE

THE APPROACH

By Terry Moore

"Light precedes every transition. Whether at the end of a tunnel, through a crack in the door or the flash of an idea, it is always there, heralding a new beginning."
–Theresa Tsalaky

IT WAS A dynamic church with quality preaching, powerful worship, and a thriving community. As an independent church plant, they were growing quite fast and enjoying the fruits of increase. The ministry was firing on all cylinders and it seemed that nothing could slow them down. The congregation multiplied and so did their impact in the community. By all metrics, we would call this particular church a *flourishing church*.

The trouble began, however, when the senior pastor developed health issues. Heart surgeries kept him in and out of the hospital, and extended leaves meant the pulpit was supplied by guest ministers and a crop of in-house speakers. He eventually reached a point where he simply could not forge ahead in the lead role and went about transitioning the church to someone else. Given that he had raised up a spiritual son in the house, succession should not have spelled disaster for the church. It did, though. Numbers declined and involvement dropped in the congregation. Staff had to be cut, and eventually, the church's impact was dissolving before their eyes.

The reason for this is important to highlight. While the new pastor *did* cut his teeth at this particular ministry, he had a *completely* separate vision for where the church should be going in the years ahead. He did not want to subtly shift the church's style; he wanted to up-end the church's very DNA.

The 180-degree change in focus, emphasis, culture, and calling was too much for the congregation to take. It was a pill they could not swallow, so they spat out the ideas wholesale. When the founding pastor noticed the severe decline, he came back to patch up the situation in an effort to return the church to its former health, but it was too late. The church never recovered. With the plummet in numbers, the church eventually liquidated as an organization and closed its doors. Staff was dismissed, the building was sold, and the proceeds went to support missionaries.

It is a cautionary tale and a stark reminder that

healthy things can be destroyed by unhealthy transitions. This rings true in church, business, marriage, and beyond. Over the years, I have seen and experienced many shifts. On a number of occasions, I was brought in to discuss transition with a church, acting as a sort of pastoral mediator between all parties involved. From that place, I have seen organizations collapse and I've seen them thrive through the whirlwind of change. I've watched churches grow tenfold and I've seen them decrease by the same multiple. On an individual level, we have witnessed believers take unexpected transitions on the chin and move ahead in grace and love. On the other hand, we have seen folks destroyed by the unexpected. If we can achieve anything with this book, it is to mimic what worked and steer clear of what didn't.

Benjamin Franklin famously said, "Nothing is certain except death and taxes." While I would agree, I would also add that *change* is yet another certainty we all experience. We know that babies, toddlers, and children are changing so fast that if we blink, we miss it. Yet even as adults, we are undergoing constant change. In fact, about 330 billion of your cells are replaced daily. That means in roughly ninety days, 30 trillion cells will have replenished—the equivalent of an entirely new you.[2] God has built change into our beings at a molecular level. Spiritual, emotional, relational, financial, and circumstantial change are every bit as unstoppable.

The question is, how do we make the most of it?

The truth is, our *approach* to transition determines how effectively and efficiently we get to the other side of it. Your *mindset* about change determines if you will experience *consequences* or *rewards* when your transition is through. In Mark's gospel, we find a flagship story that displays the process of transition and how to approach it mentally. Jesus had been teaching extensively near the waters of Galilee to the multitudes. When He wrapped up His sea-side seminar, the Bible says, "On the same day, when evening had come, He said to them, 'Let us cross over to the other side'" (Mark 4:35).

Transition began the moment the words, "Let us cross over," came out of His mouth. This marked a major shift, not just in geography but in the target audience of Jesus' ministry. They were heading to Gadarenes, which was near the southern tip of Galilee. Waiting for them there was a demonized man who lived in a graveyard, slicing himself with stones and crying out day and night. He would be gloriously delivered from a legion of demons and revival would break loose in the area. Yet between "let us cross over" and this miraculous deliverance was a transition that had to be navigated. Mark describes their time on the water this way:

> "And a great windstorm arose, and the waves beat into the boat, so that it was already filling. But He was in the stern, asleep on a pillow. And they awoke Him and said to Him, 'Teacher, do You not care that we are

perishing?' Then He arose and rebuked the wind, and said to the sea, 'Peace, be still!' And the wind ceased and there was a great calm. But He said to them, 'Why are you so fearful? How is it that you have no faith?'" (Mark 4:37-40)

We probably cannot overestimate the severity of this storm. Several of the disciples were commercial fishermen who would have been very comfortable on a sea with choppy waters. Even these men who were well-versed in nautical storms thought they were going to die! Notice the stark contrast between how Jesus and His disciples experienced this time in transit. The storm was the same for everyone, but it was not *experienced* the same by everyone. Transition is experienced uniquely by all parties involved. For Jesus, it was a chance to nap. For the disciples, it was a time to shake in their boots and worry about death.

The passage clearly demonstrates that the way you approach transition determines how you *experience* that transition. For Jesus, the transition was simply another moment to trust the Father as He rested for what was waiting on the other side of His obedience. The disciples, however, had traded their faith for fear. They had gotten their eyes on circumstances when they should have kept them on the Master, who was snoozing in the stern. This does not mean that the shortcut to navigating transition is just to nap your way through it. However, it does mean that *trust* is the best facilitator of transition. If you are not in a place of trust, you will invite all sorts of anxiety, stress, and tension into the process.

We know that everything that Jesus said and did was directed by the Father (see John 5:19). When we get a word from God at the onset, we can shift our trust to it and Him, and suddenly our path is paved with God's promises. Nothing is left to chance.

Transitions are not all created equal. Some are smooth and effortless, while others are difficult and tumultuous. A bad transition can derail even the most well-intentioned plans, leaving individuals feeling lost and uncertain about their future and confused over what went wrong. Over and over, the Bible provides a tried and true framework for how to remedy that.

MOVING TROOPS

Early on, I had to learn the art of biblical transition as my very entry into the ministry was birthed by an unexpected shift. I would be remiss to discuss transition without first unpacking my own evolution in ministry. During college, my area of study was finance, which primed me for a career in business, first starting in the real estate business. With several partners who were friends or acquaintances, we negotiated shopping centers in the Addison and North Dallas area, some of which are still standing, and some have been replaced by newer construction and tenants. In addition to retail properties, I listed and sold ranch properties, which I enjoyed very much. I love land and ranches and still enjoy looking at properties on the market or being sold. The bigger, the better! After real estate took a downturn, I turned my sights to oil and gas exploration and production. I had wells in various areas of Texas and enjoyed identifying the sites, drilling the well, managing the production, and finally decommissioning the well. So, to say that I am a bit of a pioneer is probably an understatement.

I had attended church all my life, being raised as a good Southern Baptist. At the time, we were attending a Bible Church and were faithful in small groups and participating in the church, which I believe is vital to being a follower of Jesus. The Holy Spirit was being poured out in an impactful way, across many denominations. It was in 1982 that Susan and I, along with four other couples, attended a meeting hosted by James Robison of Life Outreach International. I couldn't tell you how it happened, but all I know is that I was baptized by the Holy Spirit in a life-changing way, and I have never been the same since. As we all returned from that weekend conference, we knew that something incredible had happened to us, and it changed our world. We began having small meetings in our home, inviting whoever wanted to attend, and began to share our experience with others. We saw many miracles, people's lives changed, and people healed physically and spiritually. It was a wonderful season of personal growth as we explored Spirit-filled living.

Talks of formalizing a church began, and in all honesty, I had no interest in starting one. My wife can testify that starting a church was not in our top 100 list of things we wanted to do. At the time, our gathering was a simple Bible study, and I intended to keep it that way. We had small index cards made which said, "Terry and Susan Moore, 7:30 p.m. on Wednesdays," with our address and a small map. The other side of the card was inscribed with Psalm 100:4-5: "Enter into His gates with thanksgiving, and into His courts with praise. Be thankful to Him, and bless His name. For the Lord is good; His mercy is everlasting, and His truth endures to all generations."

With encouragement from the group and from trusted leaders, I began to seriously consider the implications of shifting from the business world to pastoral ministry. I began to see that this small gathering *could* be a church *if* the Lord willed it. After times of extended prayer and seeking, I heard God say, "Feed My sheep and shepherd My flock." He then added, "They are *My* sheep, not yours—and don't forget it."

Armed with a word from heaven, we began Sojourn Church. God did not tell me to "become a pastor." I may have been looking for a title, but He gave me a job description instead. The term "pastor" is actually used very little in the New Testament; however, the Scriptures repeatedly speak of the tasks, the sacrifice, and the servitude involved in the pastorate. God is more interested in how you feed His sheep than He is the title they address you by. As I shifted to ministry, I did so with the mentality of a steward rather than an owner. This was and continued to be my approach. I did not own the church, the ministry, nor the people. I was simply installed by God to look after and tend to them.

God wastes nothing. My time in the oil business was not wasted but intentional on God's part, and this experience built itself into my ministry and spiritual leadership. I knew from business that the key to success was putting one foot in front of the other and just being *steady*. I did not enter ministry with some grandiose vision and plan to take the world by storm. I simply wanted to move right along with God in the new thing He was doing.

My approach to this transition was not a solo affair. We were aided by a great network of leaders and people who encouraged us along the way. As time went on, we locked arms with the likes of Mike Bickle, Paul Cane, Rick Joyner, Cindy Jacobs, and countless others. Many of the household names in the prophetic movement were getting their starts in those days, and we ran alongside them. As we rubbed shoulders with them throughout the 1980s, the DNA of our church was developed.

In the early 1990s, we hosted "March for Jesus" in Dallas. We continued that for the next four years, preaching and worshiping on the streets, joined by other churches and many believers. In 1995, we caught wind of revival breaking out in Toronto. Miracles, healings, and extended times of worship were unfolding. Masses flocked to the place from around the world. Area business owners whose voicemails used to say, "Leave a message and I'll get back with you," were now saying, "Leave a message, but I might not *ever* get back with you. We are having revival over here!"

John and Carol Arnott were six weeks into this outpouring when we first attended. We sensed that what was happening was authentic and we wound up making several return trips over the years that it continued.

We went on to sponsor Catch the Fire events 1995-1997, hosted conferences such as Light the Nation, and befriended many leaders in the movement. We had already been doing work behind the Iron Curtain and eventually got plugged into what God was doing in South America, as well.

The tapestry of our church has been stitched together through a broad range of relationships. In 2002, we came into Bethel's orbit and became part of a network of pastors hosted by Bill Johnson. We saw several members go to BSSM (Bethel's School of Supernatural Ministry) and stayed in close relationship to what the Lord was doing in Redding, California, as they were experiencing a tremendous move of God in the younger generation. As Sojourn Church grew, we found ourselves brushing up against the banks of many movements and streams.

We saw people come and go, we developed teams and helped launch ministries, while ebbing and flowing with ever-changing church culture. Staff increased, procedures were developed, and we bought the property which is currently our permanent location. What never changed through the years, though, was our heart to do one thing well: disciple people. It is and has been the main thrust of the ministry.

Since 1987, I had committed myself to carrying out the call of discipleship as lead pastor of Sojourn Church. While my mandate to make disciples will never shift, the vehicle I am using to accomplish that has changed. In early 2019, during our thirty-second year in existence as a church, God commenced a major undertaking.

For years, I had been part of the group of twenty-five pastors who would meet annually from all over the world. Bill Johnson had originally started the gathering and collected leaders from Australia, interior China, Dubai, Europe, and all over the United States. At our 2019 gathering, there was much discussion about transition—a topic I had not been particularly invested in at the time. Though I had been praying about transition for the past few years, I hadn't felt like it was approaching. By then, Bill had handed his church over to Danny Silk and Danny was in the process of handing the reins over to Bill's son. While there were no feathers ruffled or major issues with the hand-off, Danny still mentioned the difficulty of the change. He quipped, "Everyone talks about how great transition is, until you're the one getting transitioned."

Not only was Danny in transition, but several others in the gathering were discussing it, as well. This got me thinking a little more carefully about the issue. The idea of a succession plan being imminent hadn't struck me as very real prior to this. Now, though, my wheels were turning.

Shortly after this gathering, I found myself in Washington, DC, for a special presentation at a gala for my brother. He had pioneered a life in the hotel industry and had been inducted into the only two halls of fame that exist in that space. Conversations flowed and I began to realize that everyone sitting at our table had either just transitioned or would be transitioning soon. Realizing we were all close in age brought the idea close to home.

After yet another meeting in Palm Springs where I was yet again surrounded by folks who had recently transitioned, I figured it was time to sit down and pray about it. In my mind, I felt I had another five years or so as lead pastor, but in the spirit, it seemed that things were being expedited. Sure enough, I heard very clearly from the Lord, "It's time to transition."

In the traditional churches I grew up in, the pastor would leave after a few years and the denomination would call in a new one to replace him. There was a committee with deliberation and votes and finally, an announcement letting us know who the next guy was. Any time a district person showed up, we knew our pastor was about to be relocated to another area. With Sojourn, however, we came out of the Jesus movement where thousands of independent, non-denominational, charismatic-type churches were planted around the country. This has led us to where we are at large in the church today. The landscape has become very binary; we have denominational and independent churches. Before the charismatic renewal, the denomination set the vision. Today, we have numerous independent churches, many of whom are not connected, so there is no real consistency among them. This has led to a lot of transitory church members. People are always coming and going. Beyond that, in these independent settings, pastoral shifts are much less bureaucratic, which has its pros and cons. We are currently living at a time when the founding pastors of all these churches are beginning to move on from their senior positions. Succession plans are often either lacking or non-existent altogether.

When God spoke to me that it was time to transition, the last thing I wanted to do was hang on to something that was no longer mine to steward. That's a sure way to destroy an organization (and yourself) in the process. At the same time, I don't make big decisions quickly, so I followed the biblical model of getting two or three witnesses on what I was hearing. I called up our oversight and elders, told them what I was hearing, and asked for their prayers and input.

"We agree," they said unanimously, without pause. I joke that they could have at least acted disappointed or hesitated a little more. The truth is, they were picking up the same signals in the spirit. Heaven had made an announcement and the right people at the right time gave ear to the word.

I gave God my *yes sir,* and less than six weeks later, I was no longer in the role I had occupied for three decades. Chris and I will work through the details of the hand-off and pull lessons from it in the coming chapters. For now, I want to major on the approach and posture needed for a shift like this. For the sake of clarity, I'll break it down into three digestible points.

1. GET A WORD FROM GOD

Don't approach transition without first approaching the Lord. He may just have something to say that you need in order to make it. I didn't quickly step down because other people my age at a dinner party were stepping down from their roles. I took my inner thoughts to the Lord.

The truth is, transition is hard, and during the process you will encounter difficulty. It's not a matter of *if* but *when.* As difficulty arises, the only surety you have as a believer is knowing that you are smack dab in the middle of the will of God. Daniel faced lions with a smile on his face because he had a word from God. Elijah had a showdown with the prophets of Baal. Noah navigated a global flood. Job lost everything. The apostles faced martyrdom. Christ Himself bore the unimaginable weight of our sin and underwent the most brutal death imaginable.

What was the common thread with all of them? They had a word from heaven propelling them forward. Hardship is coming, whether you are in the will of God or not. That hardship is much easier to withstand when you know you are right where you belong. In this place, there is *grace* for you when you need it most. When things get tricky in transition, we become doubtful and ask ourselves questions like:

- Was this the right move?
- Did I take the right job?
- Should we have waited to sell our home?
- Is this the city we should have moved to?
- Have we launched our company too soon?

The list goes on. When things get challenging, we have a tendency to re-interpret our personal history and second-guess our decisions. Getting a word from God at the start is the one-stop remedy to this. Hearing from heaven will pull you out of the guessing game and rescue your mind from being tossed to and fro. Your circumstances might be tumultuous, but your emotional state doesn't have to be.

As we discussed in Mark 4, Jesus had a confidence and a peace that the disciples lacked. Why? He had a word that said they were crossing over to the other side. Had the disciples anchored themselves in this word about crossing over, they would have seen the storms as a slight inconvenience—not a death sentence.

Hearing from God accomplishes something else that we can't ignore. It keeps you *on time*. If you leap prematurely, you will be ill-equipped. If you leap too late, you'll miss what God had for you. Hearing and obeying keeps your transition in sync with the schedule of God. Yogi Berra said, "You don't have to swing hard to hit a home run. If you got the timing, it'll go."

Timing may not be *everything*, but it is certainly close to everything. Even the secular world understands this. There are buildings all over the country that have been converted or are sitting empty which used to be occupied by Blockbuster Video. At their height, they were the biggest movie rental franchise in the world. Nobody else came close.

As the internet blossomed, Netflix came onto the scene and allowed people to rent movies from their computers. In 2000, Reed Hastings, co-founder of Netflix, approached Blockbuster and offered to sell the company for $50 million. Blockbuster turned down the offer, apparently not seeing the unstoppable digital transition that was coming.[3]

Today, Blockbuster does not exist and Netflix is worth over $140 billion. By the time it became obvious that the $50 million offer was an absolute bargain, it was too late. Blockbuster had missed their timing and filed for bankruptcy as a result.

In the church world, one of the biggest reasons pastors hold on to their role for too long is money issues. It could be that they don't have the funds to retire, so they remain in their position far longer than they should. A paycheck is not a reason to stay in a place longer than grace permits. Others are presented with shiny opportunities elsewhere and leave behind their true calling prematurely to chase a fresh pursuit. Planting your flag and anchoring yourself to a word from God keeps you from being too late or too early.

Whether it's a multi-million dollar deal, a horizontal shift at a small business, or a decision about which school to send your children to—a word from the Spirit will fine-tune your timing and keep you grounded in God's will.

2. REMAIN HUMBLE

Humility is the linchpin of transition. You can have a word from God, faith to move mountains, and a crystal clear, written plan, but if you lack humility, pride can creep in and spoil the entire process. James wrote that, "God resists the proud, but gives grace to the humble" (James 4:6). As Christians, we are in the business of humility. We humble ourselves before God and we leave the outcomes to Him. The humble don't have to have all of the answers and solutions. They recognize that they cannot figure it all out on their own and throw themselves at the feet of Jesus. In response, God shows up with grace upon grace.

Pride can blind us to the need for change and prevent us from listening to others who have valuable insights and perspectives. This, in turn, can lead to poor decision-making, missed opportunities, and ultimately, failure. Pride will cause you to overestimate your own abilities and to underestimate God's. On the other hand, humility allows us to recognize that we don't have all the answers and that we need the help of God and others to navigate the change. It allows us to listen to feedback and learn from our mistakes. It enables us to be open to new ideas and approaches that we may not have considered prior. Change can sometimes look like venturing into uncharted territory. If there is any time to realize you don't have all the answers, it is then. Let humility be like a compass pointing you in the right direction—that direction is the feet of Jesus.

Humility has a way of keeping us flexible. Our hearts remain pliable and we better adapt to the newness God is bringing us into when we are humble. Without adaptability, our transition will be miserable and we may just make others miserable along the way. Humility is the oil in the machine that makes change work!

3. COMMUNICATE OPENLY

With a word from God in your heart, a humility-soaked attitude, and a plan for honest communication, your transition will be difficult to mess up. Communication is the antithesis of isolation. Keeping lines of discussion open will be like an IV in your spiritual arm as you navigate the change.

Jim Rohn said, "Effective communication is 20% what you know and 80% *how you feel* about what you know." Let's say, for example, that you are offered a job at a new company several states away. The workload and job description remain the same, but you'll be earning 30% more at this larger company. Beyond steps 1 and 2 (walking humbly and figuring out if God is giving you a word), the wisest thing you can do is *communicate* with others about the decision. Start with your spouse and family, if you have them. The facts of most decisions are usually pretty easy to discuss. In a case like this, you see the new job, the location, and the increase. It is the *intangibles* of the decisions that need to be talked about. As Rohn put it, it's *how you feel* about what you know. The emotional toll and expectations for all parties have to be hashed out.

For instance, you might be ready to call U-Haul and pack your bags immediately, but through open communication with your spouse, serious issues come up regarding school districts, the stability of this new company, and in-law issues. Open dialogue before, during, and after transition allows us to account for things we might not have thought of otherwise. These discussions create a safe place to talk about trade-offs and values.

Communication makes *expectations* clear to everyone involved. When Pastor Chris and I began the process of transitioning the church, one thing we prioritized was open, honest dialogue. It eliminated the guesswork and made no room for the enemy. Isolation was not an option and expectations were laid out. This was one factor of many that made the hand-off a peaceable ordeal. Of course, there are always areas we could have improved upon, and that will be the case for anyone. However, the principle of communication and expectations is critical.

If we secretly put expectations on people without communicating our position, we set them up for failure. Humans are not mind readers and you cannot behave as if they were. This is true in business, marriage, parenting, and church life. You will do a great disservice to yourself and those around you if expectations are not aired out from the get-go. Make lists, set parameters, and share the details with pertinent parties. We all dread endless, boring meetings, but the right meetings with a clear agenda can save mass amounts of heartache and headache.

When Nehemiah wanted to rebuild the wall in Scripture, he made his expectations very clear in a meeting with King Artaxerxes. This enabled the king to partner with the work financially, and it set Nehemiah up for success as he transitioned to being a divine foreman, overseeing the work God had for him. Without this honest dialogue from the start, the book of Nehemiah would have been quite short and uneventful.

THE PIONEER'S PLIGHT

These best practices for approaching transition are universal. Humility, talking things through, and trusting God's word are surefire blueprints for anyone, anywhere, anytime. The quirks and challenges of transition are not universal, however. As someone who pioneered the organization, my battles have been unique to my position. They differ from Pastor Chris' struggles, who is approaching from the point of view of a successor.

Perhaps you've pioneered something of value. Maybe you were the first in your family to graduate college or you built a company from scratch. Regardless, pioneers face unique hurdles. We break ground, try new things, start small, experiment, and stick with it. Pioneers attract a certain group of people as they start out who help establish the work and are drawn to new and exciting ventures. Every church plant and business has these early adopters who help carry the initial load. In the long run, though, many of these people leave, requiring new leadership to accomplish the mission.

During my time building, I experienced plenty of trial and error. When working from scratch, the organization can become a laboratory where you experiment and sort through what works and what does not. Fortunately, I've found that God is an expert in turning our failures into weapons. He converts our shortcomings into overcomings.

As a builder, I've had to balance my desire to maintain the original vision with the need to adapt to changing circumstances. It is a tension that we all must live with. From moment to moment, day to day, week to week, and year to year, we must maintain a healthy approach so that we can return to God what He first gave to us. Like the good steward in the parable of the talents, we want to hand over God's initial investment with plenty of interest. While pioneers know all too well how to *take off*—few have mastered the *hand-off*.

CHAPTER TWO

THE INHERITANCE

By Chris McRae

"Healthy things grow. Growing things change. Changing things challenge. Challenge forces us to trust God. Trust leads to obedience. Obedience makes us healthy. Healthy things grow..." —James Ryle

PASTOR TERRY'S HAND-OFF was my hand up. One man's former assignment is another man's next pursuit. It was a cold, clear night in Kansas when I got the call. I had been away on a hunting trip and was surprised to see Pastor Terry's name pop up so late in the day. He had discussed with me a few years earlier if I would be at all interested in taking the church one day, so when the official call came that night, I was not completely shell-shocked by the offer. It was a powerful moment, no less.

"If you are planning to ride off into the sunset and leave me here to do this alone, I don't want it," I said. "But if you stay with me and I can lean on you, I'll do it." He understood and liked the arrangement. He pointed out that in January of 2020, the church would be entering its thirty-third year in existence. The third verse of Jeremiah's thirty-third chapter comes to mind: "Call to Me, and I will answer you, and show you great and mighty things, which you do not know." The transition was bursting with a sense of newness and excitement. He pointed out that my folks were scheduled to be in town at the time and that it would be the perfect timing to pass the baton.

The crazy thing was that this hand-off would happen in just *six weeks.*

After the call, my thoughts were pulled away from the pheasant we were chasing on the plains and I stirred with a sense of anticipation. At the time, it all may have seemed abrupt. The six-week-to-senior-pastor schedule was speedy. The truth is, I was not given six weeks to prepare for the transition. Whether I knew it or not, I had been preparing for this role from the time I first entered Sojourn Church twenty-four years prior as a knuckle-headed Bible school student. You might feel unprepared or ill-equipped when God calls you to a shift. Just know that when you are surprised by a transition, God is not. He has a way of prepping you for the *suddenlies* of life before the surprise ever shows up. The clay does not always know the purpose the potter has in mind but is being shaped for that purpose regardless.

The transition was to come just before a tumultuous time in our nation's history. Not only were we about to enter a global pandemic, but racial unrest was soon to reach a fever pitch culturally. It would be a summer of rioting and protests from the Black Lives Matter movement with much attention being brought to the police and the ongoing conversation on racial reconciliation. I had not been a fan of the BLM movement since its start in 2013 and had even spoken out against many of its core values. I had cut my teeth in an environment where I knew that people were more than the color of their skin.

With that said, I could not have predicted how significant the timing was for Sojourn Church to be transitioned from a white senior pastor to a black senior pastor. Many onlookers commented on this aspect of the shift, likely wondering if this move was made in response to the cultural climate we were in regarding race. The truth is, Pastor Terry *never* saw color when he was discipling me and *never* saw color when he transitioned the church to me. It was merit-based, family-based biblical succession. Race did not make the deal nor break the deal—it was irrelevant criteria, which is how things should be. I was not qualified or disqualified by checking a racial box. This speaks to Pastor Terry's heart for keeping the main thing the main thing and reflecting the love of the Father.

Gearing up for the unknown to come, I knew I needed a word from God as I approached transition. The last chapter brought much-needed attention to this point, so I won't belabor it. I will say, though, that in baseball, a first base umpire does not *look* at the play to determine if the runner is safe or out. He is taught to focus on the base and to *listen* for the sound of the ball hitting the glove. If he hears that unmistakable leather smack before the runner's foot hits the base, he knows the call to make.

Similarly, when we are thrown into transition, we are sometimes tempted to merely look around at circumstances and draw conclusions. Instead, God wants us to look *and listen* as the play unfolds in front of us. Paul said, "While we do not look at the things which are seen, but at the things which are not seen. For the things which are seen are temporary, but the things which are not seen are eternal" (2 Corinthians 4:18). Tuning our ear to the Spirit gives us an eternal perspective that we cannot go without.

As I listened to get a word, God brought me to the story of Moses and Joshua. Believe it or not, the transition between these two biblical heroes began long before Joshua ever showed up. Unfortunately, Moses did not have a book on the subject of biblical transition authored by Terry Moore and Chris McRae to guide him; however, he did have a pivotal conversation with his father-in-law. This chat with Jethro changed everything.

RAISING TROOPS

Moses was a bit of a solo leader, a workaholic, and was strung out on the issues of the people. He alone sat as judge, ruling over the affairs of the masses. When Jethro saw how unsustainable this was, he had a heart-to-heart with Moses, saying, "The thing that you do is not good. Both you and these people who are with you will surely wear yourselves out. For this thing is too much for you; you are not able to perform it by yourself" (Exodus 18:17-18).

Not only did Jethro point out the problem, he pitched a solution. He went on to counsel Moses, instructing him to raise up leaders. He mentioned that some leaders would oversee thousands, others would oversee hundreds, and others would be in charge of dozens. While Moses had a good heart, he lacked a solid corporate structure. After giving Moses a blueprint for developing and arranging leaders, Jethro said, "If you do this thing, and God so commands you, then you will be able to endure, and all people will also go to their place in peace" (Exodus 18:23).

Notice the word *endure*. Moses' *endurance* did not come from just gritting his teeth and pushing on through. It came from godly planning. From that moment on, Moses began delegating duties and became an architect of God's government on earth. The mission was now much bigger than himself. It was about the leaders he was raising, their families, and the generations to come. Had this paradigm shift not taken place, Joshua would not have had an environment of growth to step into.

Whether by instinct or by instruction, Pastor Terry has always prioritized leadership development. One of the reasons a seemingly abrupt transition worked for us was because he had spent decades pouring into his staff and creating a culture of delegation. Joshuas don't show up because a leader crosses his fingers and clicks his heels together. Joshuas show up because they are grown and developed over time via authentic discipleship. This was certainly the case in the biblical story.

As Moses' time as an overseer went on, he noticed a difference between Joshua and the others. Moses wrote the book of Exodus as a third person autobiography, and in it he recalled, "The Lord would speak to Moses face to face, as one speaks to a friend. Then Moses would return to the camp, but his young aide Joshua son of Nun did not leave the tent" (Exodus 33:11 NIV). Joshua leaned into the process and maintained a servant's heart. Eventually, as the days of Moses began to finish up, God provided a map for their succession:

> "And the Lord said to Moses: 'Take Joshua the son of Nun with you, a man in whom is the Spirit, and lay your hand on him; set him before Eleazar the priest and before all the congregation, and inaugurate him in their sight. And you shall give _some_ of your authority

to him, that all the congregation of the children of Israel may be obedient.'" (Numbers 27:18-20 emphasis added)

In a book titled *The Joshua Portrait*, authors Clinton and Haubert point out, "Joshua's ongoing association with Moses at a mentoring level did at least two things. First, it promoted Joshua's development. Through tandem training Joshua was inculcating skills, attitudes, and values needed for top level leadership. Second, it prepared the people for Joshua's installation. Whenever they saw Moses, Joshua was not far away. This gave Joshua credibility and created a positive perception of his status."[4]

If this is not wise insight on transition in leadership, I don't know what is. It's worth noting that at the start of the shift between Moses and Joshua, God said to Moses, "You shall give *some* of your authority to him." The Lord did not drop the responsibility of the entire nation into Joshua's lap in one fell swoop. It was progressive.

In modern times, this might look like occupying an executive pastor role before taking over as senior leader. It could resemble preaching once a month before graduating to speaking every Sunday. In business, it might mean having steadily increasing budgetary control before being handed a company card with no restrictions. Maybe it's driving a family car before God gives you your own wheels. The point is, God likes to ease us into responsibility. Line upon line, here a little there a little, the Lord *promotes* us without *drowning* us.

Before the transition, Pastor Terry used to bring me to meetings where he would ask for my input. He gave me rope, which I hung myself with a time or two. He would let me take the steering wheel while he kept a foot on the brake. These little tests allowed me a taste of leadership before stepping into it fully. It was not until I assumed the role of senior pastor that I realized how much backseat driving I had done in the past. It's easy to say what you would do if you were in charge. It's something else when you're the one actually responsible for the consequences of decisions at every level. Easing into the change can be a great way to reduce chaos. Even now, several years into being senior pastor of Sojourn, Pastor Terry preaches alongside me every Wednesday night. We co-teach and complement one another's styles and sermons. He has stayed true to his word to remain in-house with me, and I still draw from him all the time. We'll talk about this more in chapter six.

As the two leaders and all of Israel geared up for the transition, Moses encouraged Joshua directly: "Be strong and of good courage, for you must go with this people to the land which the Lord has sworn to their fathers to give them, and you shall cause them to inherit it. And the Lord, He is the One who goes before you. He will be with you, He will not leave you nor forsake you; do not fear nor be dismayed" (Deuteronomy 31:7-8). Not only this, but God then reiterated the encouragement directly to Joshua once the reins had been handed over: "No man shall be able to stand before you all the days of your life; as I was with Moses, so I will be with you. I will not leave you nor forsake you" (Joshua 1:5).

As I looked, leaned, and listened for the voice of God amidst this story, I heard clearly, "As I have been with Terry, so I will be with you." Circumstances, positions, and my life as a whole were soon to change, but the faithfulness of God would not. I took comfort in these words as I pivoted into my role as a successor.

THE SUCCESSOR'S STRUGGLE

The hardships of a successor are distinctly different from those of a pioneer. Make no mistake, these kinds of challenges are not limited to pastors who are transitioning churches. That just happens to be our personal example in this book. The struggles of succession are playing out all the time in every sphere. For instance, you might be a new technician struggling to measure up to the performance of the person who held that job prior. Perhaps you've married a widower and feel a sense of comparison with their first spouse. Maybe your older sibling was a Division I athlete, meanwhile, you're struggling to make the high school starting lineup.

No matter the situation, when you are coming after another, there will be a unique set of difficulties that you're presented with. I want you to know this from the start: you are not a replacement. You are a *continuation* of the plan of God. There are no second-string servants in the kingdom.

The church in Corinth dealt with issues of pioneering, succession, and people picking favorites. Paul's response was not to join the game of playing favorites or elevating one role over another. Instead, he brought both the position of pioneer and successor under the banner of God:

> *"I planted, Apollos watered, but God gave the increase. So then neither he who plants is anything, nor he who waters, but God who gives the increase." (1 Corinthians 3:6-7)*

He then goes on to say, "Now he who plants and he who waters are one, and each one will receive his own reward according to his own labor" (1 Corinthians 3:8). Did you catch that? He described the pioneer and the successor as being *one*—not because they have the same style, same approach, or that they agree on everything. They are *one* because both exist to expand the kingdom of heaven on earth.

In the denominational world that many grew up in, the congregants were married to the denomination. Pastors would come and go, but individuals chose their church based on their allegiance to the denomination. We are now living in an independent church landscape where congregants are married to the pastor—not the organizational affiliation. In fact, people usually pick their pastor before they pick their church. Above the coffee in the foyer or even the quality of the worship set, they are choosing a preacher. This has created some trouble in modern church hand-offs, because when the pastor goes, the congregants often leave, as well. You can't throw a frisbee in the Bible Belt without hitting someone who's been through a church split of some kind.

While stepping into my new role, I knew we would lose some people. There are folks who stay, folks who stay for a little while, folks who don't give you the time of day, and folks who eventually come back. It's all to be expected. If there are shareholders who leave when a company gets a new CEO, you can guarantee there are church members who back away when a new pastor is ordained. The decision is usually stylistic rather than personal, but it can still hurt. Over the past few years, I've been blessed to hear some of the strangest excuses for people's departures. Pastor Terry would remind me, "Chris, this is all part of it. God is moving troops and He has the right to do that. Keep your eyes on Jesus."

In reality, COVID helped ease the transition because, with the church briefly shut down, many of the older people saw it as an opportunity for an easy way to depart and not come back. Conversely, because many new people had come to the church, I was able to establish myself as a leader for new people who had no context for the past.

Big shifts don't necessarily create weaknesses; they expose existing ones. Here's a metaphor: if a tire's inner tube has a leak, you can inflate it and dunk it in water. The bubbles indicate where the puncture is. That water did not create the leak, it just revealed it. Major transitions generally do not create issues within us, they just indicate the presence of issues that already exist. The quote at the beginning of chapter one says that transition brings *light*. And what does light do? It exposes. Let me encourage you to not see this as a negative thing, because exposure can lead to healing.

Insecurities are often highlighted when moving from one place to another. Promotion is a good thing, but it may mean dealing with imposter syndrome and feeling like you aren't qualified. I certainly had to deal with my own insecurities as I moved into the senior pastor spot. I was not without encouragement, though. The night Pastor Terry told me I would be taking the role, he said, "There are two people on the planet you can trust. Your father and me. Many people will have an agenda for your life. We have no agenda except your success."

I took that to heart and *oh, how true it was*. When you move into a new position, you will hear many who say, "I just want the best for you," yet you can smell the agenda coming from a mile away. The reason being, those who did not get their way for years have a new ear to speak into—a new button to push. Imagine being a brand new plant manager and having team members walk into your office on day one congratulating you and introducing themselves. By day two, those polite folks are dropping hints, asking for new policies, major purchases, or a new coffee maker for the break room. Leaders desperately need discernment and people in their corner who are completely free of all agenda. Otherwise, they will be yanked around by every request.

Dealing with preexisting teams can be a major hurdle for a new leader. You will have to navigate boards, advisors, and elders who were established by the former leader. There is a tension between honoring the existing framework and injecting newness. Some folks may need to be released and others may need to be retained. Transition is like a blender, mixing together unique styles and approaches. If handled poorly, it can be a gigantic mess. If handled effectively, the end result will be unity and solidarity. The last thing you want is to alienate your team, lose trust, and hamstring your goals.

A successor's approach to a hand-off is going to be similar to that of a pioneer. A word from God, humility, and open dialogue all have their place on this side of the aisle, as well. There are a few unique points of instruction, though, that we should consider as successors.

1. ASK THE RIGHT QUESTIONS

Jesus asked 307 questions in the gospels. He himself was only *asked* a total of 183.[5] To put this in perspective, Jesus asked twice the questions that His followers did. Being inquisitive is more Christlike than you might have realized. Of the questions that Jesus was asked, He only directly answered three in Scripture. Instead, He often answered a question with another question. It's as though Jesus was getting His audience to upgrade their questions and shift their thinking. We would do well to adopt His approach. What would it cost you to double the questions you usually ask? What might you gain from that effort?

A pioneer who has poured their blood, sweat, and tears into an organization better ask some good questions to any potential candidate. After all, you are handing over something you've invested your life into. Likewise, successors have a number of questions they ought to ask, as well.

Nobody wants to inherit a dumpster fire. We *especially* don't want to inherit a dumpster fire disguised as a thriving organization. The way we avoid this is by asking good questions at all levels of leadership. Asking questions is an admission that you do not have all the answers. An inquisitive heart is often a humble one. Questions ought to be flowing before, during, and after transition. Beforehand, you want to know what you are getting yourself into and what the expectations are. For instance, you might ask ahead of time:

- What is the organizational structure like?
- Can I read the governing documents and bylaws?
- What does success look like here?
- How are the financials/when was the last audit?
- How can I best honor the pioneer and the organization?

During the transition, while steps are being taken and implementation is happening, the questions should not dry up. Ideally, the questions don't look like the disciples' questions in Mark 4, "Don't you care that we are perishing!?" Instead, we should come prepared with well-rounded questions that keep the shift on track. For instance:

- What unexpected issues do we have and how can we solve them?
- Are there any pain points we need to address?
- Is our plan proving to be workable or does it need adjustment?
- Are we maintaining humble hearts?
- How far along are we and how far do we have to go?

You guessed it: the questions don't stop before and during transition but continue *after* you've gotten to the other side. In fact, this can be some of the most important times of inquiry you have. You could call it debriefing, project review, or something else, but it truly needs to happen.

Some years ago, the U.S. Army developed a system called AAR. This stands for After Action Review. An AAR is a process used to assess a project, event, or mission once it is completed. What does it look like? Usually a team reflects on strengths, weaknesses, performance, and areas of improvement. This line of questioning works, not just for succession plans, but for any event, new pursuit, or even regular service that your organization goes about. It may sound complex, but it's ridiculously simple and can be implemented with four questions:

- What was supposed to happen?
- What actually happened?
- Why was there a difference?
- What can we learn from this?

2. HONOR PROFUSELY

Honor is the kryptonite of competition. It keeps you out of pride, performance, and fleshly motivation. From start to finish, the Bible is rife with Scriptures on honor.

The word honor in the Greek actually means *to properly perceive the value of something.* This means when we honor something or someone, we are assigning the correct sense of worth to it. The opposite of honor would be to step into a business or ministry or family and treat it as though it had no existing value. Where honor is lacking, a business might die because a new CEO needlessly tampered with existing products without assigning value to what was built. Where honor is lacking, a blended family may experience strife because a new stepparent does not properly *value* the children from the prior marriage.

When we keep honor in mind, it acts as an anchor that guides us when we assume our new roles. Honor is not just a mental state or a heart posture. It is an action. Honor without action is just flattery. I would encourage you to think of some practical ways to honor the existing framework and/or your predecessor.

For me, I determined early on to utilize Pastor Terry's manuals that he had written over the years. In fact, Pastor Robert Morris told me before taking the church, "Preach Dad's messages. No need to reinvent the wheel. Stay close to the heart of the house." I worked to do just that. I re-preach his messages routinely with my own spin and re-tell his stories. Firstly, because they're gold. Secondly, I do not need to start from scratch. I'm building on a foundation, not pouring a new one. Honor, to me, looks like pulling from his years of study and dedication to the teaching of the Word. His insights on agape love, identity, purpose, freedom, and more have shaped my output in the pulpit.

I would encourage you also to salvage anything you can when you step into a new role. Don't clear house immediately. Repurpose existing systems and make them your own. This will be easier on your team and will demonstrate your heart to serve and honor. We have all heard stories of mergers and acquisitions that were a headache for everyone involved because of abrupt change and no honor for what was there before.

As mentioned, I wanted Terry's involvement right out of the gate. I love him like a father and never sensed any competition at all. In the midst of me honoring what he has done, he would temper this, reminding me, "Don't copy me and don't do it this way just because that's what I did. God may have something new for you." In this, we were able to balance honoring the old with ushering in the new.

3. EVALUATE TIRELESSLY

At Calvary, there were some things that stayed the same, like justification through faith. There were other things that changed, like the blessing of Abraham now reaching to the Gentiles. Finally, some things came to an end, like the requirements to fulfill ceremonial laws. What do we keep, what do we change, and what do we end? These three questions have guided so many major events in Scripture and major events in our lives. They are the cornerstone of healthy evaluation. We will unpack a little more on this in chapter eight.

As a successor, you don't have to overhaul everything all at once. You may need a fair bit of newness thrown in, yet other things might just need a few tweaks. For instance, I eliminated certain worship songs for our set that I felt were man-centered and lacked sound doctrine. This seems to be a growing trend in the church world that was not an issue that needed addressing ten years ago. Successors will deal with new cultural or market issues that the pioneer was not presented with. It's all part of the process of continual evaluation.

We alluded to Nehemiah earlier and his meeting with the king. I'd like to briefly point out the steps he took in actually rebuilding the wall once his meeting wrapped up. The first thing he did was *evaluate*. During a night ride with a few buddies, he made his way through Jerusalem and inspected the damage. He noted the aftermath of fires that had ruined the city gates and rubble that used to be standing structures (see Nehemiah 2:17). He did not have the luxury of calling an insurance adjuster and getting a check for reconstruction. It was all on him. He noted the damage, kept track of needed repairs, and built a team to get it done.

This does not mean our sole purpose in evaluation is to find out what's damaged and broken. That is only part of it. We also want to discover what is *healthy*. What is working here? What is producing the most fruit? Health matters more than growth. Healthy things grow, so seek health before you seek growth. If you try to grow something that's unhealthy, you will create a mutiny.

This chapter began with a James Ryle quote on growth that I have echoed many times in many places: "Healthy things grow. Growing things change. Changing things challenge. Challenge forces us to trust God. Trust leads to obedience. Obedience makes us healthy. Healthy things grow..." Right in the middle of this loop is the word *challenge*. Challenges, difficulties, and storms are baked into the process of change. In the coming chapter, Pastor Terry will share what to do about it.

CHAPTER THREE

THE STORMS

By Terry Moore

"Life with God is not immunity from difficulties, but peace in difficulties." —C.S. Lewis

LIGHTNING AND THUNDERSTORMS are caused by a combination of moisture, an unstable atmosphere, and temperature changes. In other words, the weather itself testifies that change and instability have a way of generating stormy, tumultuous atmospheres. I would like to propose that in the spirit, seasons of change and instability also have a way of attracting storms in our lives. During these seasons, we are disrupting patterns, breaking into new territory, and experiencing new levels of pressure, which can all drum up real difficulty.

What is it about transition that attracts the storms of life? Why is change such a magnet for problems? For starters, it's where you are most vulnerable. You have not had the luxury of settling in and fine-tuning your skill set. You lack your bearings. You are out of your comfort zone and are already dealing with underlying stress and tension. From this place, even minor inconveniences can become large hurdles.

In Acts 27, Paul is imprisoned and being carried, along with over 200 others, on a large boat. He advises that they avoid the waters by instruction from the Spirit. God was calling for a delay of their transition. Against Paul's better judgment, the crew set sail. Nevertheless, the small breeze that guides their sail becomes a gale-force wind called the Northeaster that nearly drowns everyone on the boat. They fight for their lives for two weeks until landing on Malta. Being in transition on the waters meant they had limited resources, limited mobility, and dire consequences if things went south—and they most certainly did. Likewise, when we are moving from point A to point B, we often have a limited budget and perspective. Failure can be hugely consequential. Storms are challenging by nature but even more so when you are away from what's familiar. Despite this, God has given us ways to shore up our lives in the midst of transitional vulnerability.

IDENTIFY THE SOURCE

Have you ever awakened to find a leak in your house? It could be a flooded basement or water pooling up in the kitchen. The first question we ask is: *Where on earth is this water coming from?* We check for broken pipes, loose fittings, and leaks in the ceiling. Why? If we don't identify the source of the leak, we can't stop the leak. This critical step comes before cleanup and repair.

In the medical community, a treatment path cannot be administered until the source of the ailment is identified. In corporate management, a company's culture cannot be improved until the bad actors are pointed out and dealt with. We could list endless examples from many spheres, but the point is simple: when the source is recognized, we are able to manage the crisis and develop a path forward. The storms in your life have a source, and your methods for dealing with them change depending on where the storm is coming from.

SOURCE #1: THE STORM FROM GOD

Now and then, God creates or allows for strenuous circumstances in our lives. This is not a means of punishment nor is it some sort of divine cruelty. In fact, the endgame of these storms is our betterment. They are a course correction, a sacrifice, or a nudge to get back on track. In the midst of the challenge, it might seem awful, yet God is working out a master plan for our good. For instance, Jonah was called by God to preach in the city of Nineveh. The very next verse states that Jonah then "headed for Tarshish" (Jonah 1:3).

I'm no Hebrew scholar, but Tarshish does not sound like Nineveh to me. Jonah was running, not just from his calling, but from the presence of the Lord. During his disobedient transition, he found himself on a boat heading south. When a massive storm came, Jonah figured he was the bad apple and asked the sailors to throw him overboard. It was a suicide attempt. It was then that he became fish food. He remained there for three days before being spat out onto dry land where he had the choice to pick up where he left off with his calling.

We may be tempted to think that being in the belly of a whale was some punishment on God's part for Jonah. In fact, the opposite is true. When Jonah was swallowed up by the whale, he was really being swallowed up by the mercy of God. The circumstances might not have been pleasant and he would certainly regard it as a storm, but it was the *grace* of God to give him a second chance.

This does *not* mean that God is the architect of all storms in our lives, as we will see in the coming points. It does not mean that God is using sickness as a teaching tool or destroying marriages to prove a point. However, it does mean that when difficulty arises, it's important to stop and discern whether or not it is God getting you back on track. Is it the Lord ordering or allowing circumstances to pull you into your destiny? Is it God saving you from yourself? There are numerous inmates sitting in prison currently who admit that their arrest and incarceration, as stormy and difficult as the process might have been, was an act of the mercy of God. Why? Had they not been locked up, they'd be dead in the streets.

God is known to prune our lives (see John 15). He specializes in this as our Master Gardener. This means He cuts away things that are unfruitful to make room for growth. If we are being honest with ourselves, this pruning often feels like a storm—especially when lots of things are pruned in a short period! Nevertheless, God is working out a final result that will better your life, advance His purposes, and further establish the kingdom on earth.

SOURCE #2: THE STORM FROM THE ENEMY

Jesus gave us a succinct and clear job description of the enemy when He said, "The thief comes *only* to steal and kill and destroy" (John 10:10 NIV, emphasis added). Satan has no other existence but that of a thief, a destroyer, and a killer. If a storm has hit your life and it looks like theft, unjust loss, and destruction, you are likely dealing with an attack from the wicked one.

Entire volumes have been written on the subject of demonic attack and spiritual warfare, so I won't attempt to compete with those here. I will, however, echo Paul's words when he said, "Satan might not outwit us. For we are not unaware of his schemes" (2 Corinthians 2:11). If we are *ignorant* of the devil's devices, we will be *susceptible* to those devices. It is critical that we flow in the discernment of spirits (see 1 Corinthians 12:10), recognizing what is demonic and what is not.

Things like a loss of spiritual desire, confusion, constant negativity, or desire for self-harm are all hallmarks of a storm from the enemy. Doubt, shame, guilt, and despair are all the devil's doing. When a gift from God is under attack, you can bet the enemy has his hand involved.

It's also important to note that *anyone* could undergo an attack from the enemy. This does not mean that you are out of the will of God or that you are somehow being punished. According to Ephesians 6, all of us as believers are in the same wrestling match with principalities, powers, and rulers of the air. The good news is that we have been equipped with authority over all the power of the enemy (see Luke 10:19).

Satan walks about like a roaring lion seeking whom he may devour (see 1 Peter 5:8). We may hear the roars or see the lion; we simply will not fear his bite. As children of God, we are undevourable!

SOURCE #3: THE STORM FROM PEOPLE

We are sometimes tempted to think that every bad thing that happens is a demonic attack. The truth is, people can be pretty good at messing things up without the devil's help. In Scripture, we have numerous examples of troublemakers, thorns in the flesh, distractors, and agitators who create chaos for others—whether it's Paul saying, "Alexander the metalworker did me a great deal of harm" (2 Timothy 4:14 NIV) or David writing, "Those who hate me without reason outnumber the hairs of my head" (Psalm 69:4).

Some people will make *their* problems *your* problems, while others will generously create fresh baked problems from scratch for you. This does not mean that everyone is out to get you or that storms created by people are always intentional. Sometimes they're not. Only God is perfect, and as humans, we are quite good at proving that.

For instance, on the set of Mel Gibson's movie *The Patriot,* the crew was shooting a massive battle scene with horses, full battalions marching in the distance, shots being fired, and cannons going off. It was a giant undertaking with hours spent setting up and orchestrating the shot. When the camera was rolling, one of the extras was going to briefly cross in front of Mel Gibson's character on horseback—which he did. The problem was, he was wearing a full colonial infantry costume complete with the wig, a haversack, a rifle, *and* a pair of Oakley sunglasses, which he had forgotten to take off. The entire scene had to be shot again, costing an additional $10,000.

Whether mistakes are intentional or innocent, our heart posture is to remain in a place of patience, understanding, and forgiveness. If we want to enjoy a world where people can benefit and bless us, we also have to accept that those same people can bring headaches and storms into our lives, as well.

SOURCE #4: THE STORM FROM OURSELVES

Three young men were swimming in a lagoon on spring break when two of them noticed their buddy was struggling to tread water. At the shore, they got the lifeguard's attention. Looking out at the flailing swimmer, the lifeguard, surprisingly, did not move. The two friends began to shout, "What are you doing? Our friend is drowning, jump in after him!"

Yet the lifeguard waited and waited. The swimmer struggled, slapped the water, and paddled recklessly. Finally, after several minutes, the swimmer's arms stopped flailing and his head went underwater. Immediately, the lifeguard dove in after him. After pulling him to shore, the two friends rebuked the lifeguard again, "Why did you wait so long? He almost drowned!"

To this, the lifeguard replied, "I had to wait for him to give up. I couldn't save him until he stopped trying to save himself." Had the lifeguard dove in after the frantic young man, the rescue would be botched and he could have taken the lifeguard down with him.

When we get to the end of ourselves, we get to the start of God's grace. So many of the problems we create in our own lives are because we are still trying to do it all ourselves. We have not given up and let God do what He does best. We are splashing, struggling, panting, and all the while, preventing supernatural power from taking hold in our lives.

A storm that comes from ourselves is one of the more obvious sources on the list, yet we sometimes fail to properly acknowledge this. Nobody likes to see their own blemishes. Right after the fall of man, Eve blamed the devil, and Adam blamed Eve, but nobody fessed up and took personal responsibility. This pattern has been true ever since.

Similar to the previous point, not all self-imposed storms happen because of bad motives. We all know the saying, "The road to hell is paved with good intentions." I have certainly seen big issues arise from well-meaning endeavors. When we first started the church, so much of everything was based on trial and error. This often led to *errors* that created *trials*. For instance, I got real spiritual early on and decided I would stop taking up offerings so we could spend more time praying for people. I figured if we wanted more time to prophesy and lay hands on folks, we could steal that time from the in-service offering.

A missionary came to the church during that season and spoke. We paid him an honorarium from our church funds, but of course, did not receive a public offering. While driving him back to the airport, he asked about it, "I noticed you didn't take up an offering for the church."

"Right. We stopped doing that."

"Why?"

"So we could have more time to pray for people and do ministry."

He paused at my explanation, then asked, "Did God tell you to do that?"

I pulled at my collar and started driving a little quicker. Uncomfortable and anxious, I had to admit, "Well... no."

"I understand where you're coming from," he said. "The people who have a revelation of giving would give if you put the offering plate on top of the roof. They would find a way to get there and give. But there are people who don't have that understanding and need to be taught. You can pray for them all day, but they need instruction."

I repented and began normal offerings again the very next Sunday. I was in the lab experimenting without a denominational pattern to follow. While my intentions were fine, I needed to correct course and admit fault. If you have pain points in your life, I would encourage you to take inventory and see how much of it is directly tied to your own actions and choices. This does not mean we get caught up in shame, guilt, or condemnation. Instead, it means we recalibrate and avoid these preventable storms in moving ahead.

PAUL'S AFFLICTIONS

Paul was one of the most transient people in the Bible. He seemed to always be in transition from one city to the next or from one ministry emphasis to another. There are nearly sixty cities and regions in the Scriptures that are directly connected with Paul. He lived on the move and was all too familiar with the storms that can come with shifts.

He had experienced trials from the enemy. On one occasion, he wrote to the Thessalonians, "For we wanted to come to you—certainly I, Paul, did, again and again—but Satan blocked our way" (1 Thessalonians 2:18). On other occasions, he knew that God was blocking the way and could not visit particular areas because the Holy Spirit forbade it (see Acts 16:16). People also generated storms for Paul, in some cases quite literally, as we see in Acts 27:21. Last but not least, Paul got in his own way at times. In Acts 21:4 and 11, Paul is warned by the Holy Spirit to not go down to Jerusalem to preach. Why? Because Paul was originally called to the Gentiles. Yet he had such a heart for his people that he ignored the prophetic warning and was arrested in short order. Many scholars agree that while Paul had persecution coming his way, he experienced unnecessary amounts of it at times because of his zeal.

Paul went through storms from God, storms from the enemy, storms from people, and storms from himself. Yet through them all, the overarching message of his life was the glory of the crucifixion and resurrection of the Lord Jesus Christ. He had his eyes on something greater than the storm at hand. As we adopt this approach, we will not be insulated from trials, but we will know how to navigate them with peace and hope.

There is no doubt that Paul's Christ-centered worldview empowered him as he endured the storms of life and ministry. But do we have that same worldview? Barna recently reported that only 37% of pastors in America have a biblical worldview.[6] The others surveyed hold to a mixed worldview that incorporates other religions, dogmas, and ideologies. Given this, it's no wonder we have so many problems in society. When the pulpit is void of sound teaching, society is void of godly influence.

In Matthew 13, Jesus speaks of the wheat and tares. The two crops are growing alongside each other simultaneously. Wheat and tares are impossible to tell apart until they start putting out seeds. We are beginning to see the seed that is being put out in culture. We can tell who is legitimate and who is not. The difference between true and false is becoming ever clearer. Malachi prophesied of the last days and said, "And you will again see the distinction between the righteous and the wicked, between those who serve God and those who do not" (Malachi 3:18).

God is shifting the troops, sending laborers, and raising up those who will hold to the Word and power of God. This means we are not just going to have meetings to have meetings. It means we are going to see the impact of the kingdom trickle into every corner of the culture.

As we transition into this role as the body of Christ, know that it will not be without road bumps, delays, difficulties, and frustrations. In Mark 4, the storm in the midst of the transition was a chance for Jesus to provide a teachable moment on faith. In Matthew 14, the disciples were transitioning away from the crowd to the other side of the lake when Peter walked on water. While the storm distracted him, it did not drown him, and he was able to experience a miracle that those in the boat did not.

Don't allow the potential storms of transition to keep you from what God has for you. You are taking a risk if you stay and you are taking a risk if you go. Ultimately what wins the day is getting a green light from the Lord and navigating the path ahead with a humble heart.

RESPONSES AND REACTIONS

When chaos hits, our task is to discover the origin of the storm and act accordingly. If the storm is due to the fact that God removed negative influences from your life and is calling you to higher sacrifice, rebuking the devil won't help you. If the storm is because you mishandled your finances, blaming your boss won't suffice. If the enemy is eating your lunch, giving God credit for the destruction won't honor Him and it won't help you.

Because we now know that storms will make their way to us from a variety of sources, it's all the more important that we know *how* we will respond when the storm comes. What's your plan? How will you navigate the inevitable? We are not called to *react* to the difficulties. We are called to respond to them. What's the difference between the two? See chart below:

Reaction	Response
Short-sighted	Mindful of the long-term
Emotionally driven	Measured and thoughtful
Impulsive	Well-planned
Biased	Objective
Lacks balance	Considerate and wise
Prayerless	Prayerful
Powerless	Powerful

Reactions resemble firing from the hip. This might work on rare occasions, but ultimately you want a proper *response*. This means you know how you will respond before the storm clouds ever begin to appear. You want your answer confirmed in your heart before the question is ever posed. We will talk more about transition planning in chapter five, but for now, I will say this: factor trouble into your plan. Build headache into the expectations. No transition will ever be seamless. If you can settle that before you start, you will not be shocked by the storm; instead, you will speak peace to it.

CHAPTER FOUR

THE MYTHS

By Chris McRae

"*Beware of false knowledge; it is more dangerous than ignorance.*" —*George Bernard Shaw*

IT WAS OUR first major conference since I had stepped into the senior pastor position. We had planned for weeks, brought in speakers, had a set schedule, and covered the event in prayer. What could go wrong? With these ducks in a row, we were slated to have the *perfect* gathering. The problem is, perfect conferences don't actually exist on this side of heaven. Murphy's law came into play and everything that could have gone wrong went wrong. From streaming issues to schedule problems and staff concerns, the entire thing was a hot mess.

In the midst of troubleshooting and running around

trying to get things in order, Pastor Terry walked by me and said, "Nothing like being in charge, huh?" and casually strolled off smiling ear to ear. All I could do was laugh.

Before ever taking this role, he had said to me, "You're going to feel the weight of this office once you step into it." I thought I knew what that weight might feel like, but I truly did not. It hits you in a very real way once the shift actually occurs. Whether you have transitioned into a marriage, parenthood, a new business, or a promotion, you often have no way of fully preparing for the weight of responsibility that comes with it. When you are in charge, your off-hand ideas become instructions to your team, because your words carry a weight that they didn't before. The organization's failures become your personal failures because the buck stops with you. Your mood becomes an atmosphere as your employees or your children are orbiting around your demeanor. Everything you do or say has a little more *oomph* to it.

I had certainly underestimated all of the nuances and responsibilities that would come with this role. At the same time, I overestimated other things. With any transition, we are prone to miscalculating and misunderstanding how things will play out. In this chapter, we'll bust through some of these myths and provide clarity on what to expect and what not to expect during the transition process.

MYTH #1: TRANSITION IS ALWAYS SMOOTH

Given that the name of the previous chapter is "The Storms," I would hope we have busted this myth at this point in the book. It is worth noting, though, that even the most well-thought-out, well-executed, and divinely-conceived transition plan will still have potholes and road bumps. Plans are crucial, as you will see in the next chapter, but they do not insulate you from glitches and problems. Transition is messy, unpredictable, and full of the unexpected. For instance, you might have the most glorious and organized transition laid out for moving your family from Memphis to St. Louis. You've crossed every *t* and dotted every *i*. Yet when you arrive to pick up the U-Haul, you find a squirrel has chewed through your hitch cables and the trailer has no lights.

Perhaps you planned a five-year retirement goal with a savings schedule that puts you right where you need to be to enjoy your golden years. Then, by year three of that plan, the company files bankruptcy and you are on your own to bridge the gap. Good plans can help our journey but will never *perfect* it. Here's an oxymoron for transition: Expect the unexpected and don't be surprised by surprises. The suddenlies of life have a way of stealing our peace if we let them. Continue to press into the One who makes the crooked path straight.

The main point I want to drive home is this: just because things are difficult does not mean the transition was not the will of God. In fact, some of the most challenging transitions have eventually led to the most glorious outcomes. When we feel pressed or the process gets hard, it's tempting to question, "Was God even in this move?"

Think about the transition that occurred in Acts 2 when Jesus ascended to heaven and the Holy Spirit fell, causing the kickstart of the global church. We can all agree that this transition was unequivocally the will of God, but think about the pain and problems that were coming through this transition. Nearly every early church leader for the next several decades would be killed by the government. Church gatherings were from house to house, often avoiding the authorities. Imprisonment and beatings would be the norm for those who professed faith in Jesus. Now, you might think, *Well, sure Chris, those were challenges. But those were challenges from outside the church.*

Glad you brought it up! Let's talk about the problems *within* the church. Heresy was rampant. Gnostics who taught that Christ did not physically rise from the dead were pulling many away from the true faith. Entire churches and church leaders were prone to classism and playing favorites. Ministers began preaching the gospel for money's sake. A council met in Jerusalem to hash out a host of doctrinal disagreements. The cherry on top was a couple being struck dead for lying about financial commitments to the church. The list goes on.

Was the church the will of God? Absolutely. Did it come with a slew of issues both outside and inside the church? You better believe it. Difficulty should not cause us to question the will of God. It should cause us to press into it all the more. Transition will never be perfectly smooth.

MYTH #2: EVERYONE WILL BE FOR THE TRANSITION

Steve Jobs said, "If you want to make everyone happy, don›t be a leader, sell ice cream." When you institute change, it won't please everyone. When we brew up a creative strategy or a necessary change, we are so mesmerized by it that we think everyone else will be, too. This is simply not the case. You may have spent the afternoon drumming up the most air-tight and robust argument imaginable as to why you can and *should* buy a boat. This does *not* mean that your spouse is going to instantly throw on a lifejacket, eager to make your dreams come true.

There are those who will be against the transition and need some time to come around. There are others who are against the transition and will *never* come around. You cannot please everyone. People are resistant to change, not necessarily because they are stubborn knuckleheads. Often, they are hardwired for it. With the risk of sounding overly technical, the part of your brain that is responsible for your survival is called the amygdala. This little area in the back of your head releases adrenaline and causes you to either fight or run when things get dangerous. Beyond that, the amygdala actually interprets change as a threat.[7] In other words, your own brain wants to protect you from change. This is why so many people in an organization, when presented with a new idea—even a solid one—will resist it.

"What's not to love?" we say, after pitching a new idea. As leaders, we can be idealistic in believing that our vision is the most lovable path on the planet. We all know the stories of pastors who came into a church and started teaching things that ran against the tradition and theological history of that body. While the pastor had planned to lead that congregation in a mighty revival, he usually ended up leaving the congregation with termination papers in hand.

Why does this sort of rejection and resistance happen? Often it's because people fail to *see* what we see. Whether you're dealing with family, co-workers, or your own employees, learn to communicate your vision plainly. People can overcome their hesitations when they see a valid reason to. Emphasize the need, the purpose, and the motivation behind the change you're bringing about. If you are pulling your children from public school to private, lay out a giant list of reasons that all point to the fact that you love them and want the best for them. If you are shutting down your business and have to let employees go, spell out exactly why and demonstrate how this is the best or only long-term solution.

When my transition took place at the church, there were those who resisted the transition and left, which was not easy. We keep the door open, though, because they may come back. Ultimately, transitions are almost never unanimously accepted. When a new president takes office, about half the country is usually ticked off. When the CEO of a major company steps down, shareholders sell and the stock price can take a hit. As we move from place to place and purpose to purpose, we will rarely have 100% buy-in from those close to us. What we will have, however, is the surety that comes from being in the dead-center of the will of God.

MYTH #3: EVERYONE WILL BE AGAINST THE TRANSITION

On the flip side, insecurity can have us convinced that the whole world is against us. You could call this the victim mentality. In this headspace, we believe that everyone is shooting holes in everything that we are doing and saying. It is paranoia that's based on a lie. If we buy into this thinking, it'll keep us from shifting and moving into the next phase that God has for us.

Think about the company Apple, for example. Many people today don't realize that through the '90s, Apple was slowly dying. They had created the personal computer, but competitors were outdoing them with cheaper options. As a solution, Steve Jobs developed concepts like the iPod and eventually the iPhone and iPad. They could have assumed the market wouldn't trust new devices from a failing tech company. They could have assumed no one would be on board with the change. Instead, they went for it, and today the business is worth nearly $3 trillion.

We tend to overestimate the blowback we are going to get, especially if we are prone to overthinking. While there will always be some resistance, it›s important to recognize that you will have many advocates rooting for you. There will be supporters of the transition who can help to move things forward. It›s important to identify and engage with these individuals while also addressing the concerns of those who may not be on board. To those who truly are against any given transition, hear them out. Be willing to learn from those who disagree with you. Be willing to take notes and make adjustments as needed.

One way that this "everyone is against me" mentality manifests is through a sense of loneliness. When we step into a new place, we may sense a lack of support or that we are laboring alone. Elijah certainly felt this as he was standing up against the prophets of Baal. In fact, he announced to the people, "I alone am left a prophet of the LORD; but Baal's prophets are four hundred and fifty men" (1 Kings 18:22). He felt outnumbered. It seemed that those who were against him were more than those who were for him. However, just one chapter later, the Lord made it clear that Elijah was not alone in his righteousness, but there was a remnant of 7,000 others who had not bowed their knees to Baal (see 1 Kings 19:18).

Never allow the possible rejection of man to keep you from the approval of God. If the Lord wills it, don't scrap it. Your prediction that "so and so will not be happy about this" may or may not be an accurate one. Regardless, your job is not to weigh your obedience against the reactions of people. Your job is to remain in obedience regardless of the reactions of people.

You will have supporters and protestors. You will have advocates and persecutors. You will have encouragers and detractors. You may even have some who are in between. Despite it all, our role is to own what God has given us and communicate it with excellence.

MYTH #4: TRANSITION IS THE END OF PURPOSE FOR THE PREDECESSOR

A good predecessor's work will outlive their tenure. Their foundation will continue to provide support for new people, ideas, and pursuits. If you have handed over a thriving business, that company will be indebted to your work as long as it exists. If your children are now having kids of their own, your purpose has not ended—it's just shifted.

The seeds of encouragement, love, guidance, discipline, and wisdom will continue to grow in perpetuity, even though your role looks different. You've probably heard some version of the first law of thermodynamics: energy cannot be destroyed, only converted from one form to another. I believe this is true of our purpose in Christ: it cannot be destroyed, only changed. This very topic will be teased out in more detail in chapter seven by Pastor Terry.

MYTH #5: TRANSITION IS CONVENIENT

Change is expensive. It will cost you time, talent, and treasure. You will pour out resources, work late nights, and have early mornings dedicated to any meaningful change. The word value inherently means that something is worth a high price. If the result of a transition is valuable, then it absolutely will cost you something to get there. If it did not cost you, it was not valuable.

If we are being honest, we love our routines. We drive the same route to work, we eat the same types of meals, we scroll the same apps, and we sleep on the same side of the bed. Routines are comfortable, convenient, and allow us to be productive without spending any extra mental energy on our daily decisions. Transition takes an ax to our routines. Major shifts in life break up the monotony of our schedules and rip us out of the comfortable, convenient ruts we've spent so much time in.

This does not come easy but is necessary. We all know routines have to change for change to truly last.

One of the top-selling self-help books of all time, *Atomic Habits*, is dedicated to the topic of changing our routines. In fact, the book is all about how to make those changes *easier*. While we can certainly apply principles that make change more manageable, there is no secret formula to make change *convenient* every time.

The timing of transition is one of the major inconveniences. Maybe you would have liked to have a little more of a buffer, but the market is calling you to launch your company now. Perhaps you are eager to graduate high school early and head off to college, but your folks are pulling back the reins. God's timing is always best for you and your future, but it may feel inconvenient at the time.

One of the major inconveniences of transition is the need to acquire new skill sets. Routines are so easy to stay in because we've mastered the ins and outs of our jobs and responsibilities. Without newness on the table, we don't have to gain new skills and tools. However, when God shifts us, we are sometimes starting from zero and working our way through new skills and knowledge. Get comfortable being the newbie. Get comfortable being the least qualified person in the room.

Paul wrote, "[Love] bears all things, believes all things, hopes all things, endures all things" (1 Corinthians 13:7). Notice the first list item, "Love bears all things." As Christians, we are bearing/carrying many things at once. Jesus Himself instructed us to carry our cross. The temptation, though, is to put the cross down when the going gets tough. The Bible calls us to "bear one another‹s burdens," for instance (see Galatians 6:2). Does this mean that when we are bearing someone's burden, we get to drop our own? Is Paul saying that when I'm helping a friend in his struggle, I get to stop being a husband and a dad? Of course not! It means when I'm bearing someone's burden, it is in *addition* to my own.

This is the opposite of convenient.

Helping someone carry their cross for a season does not mean I drop mine. It simply means I have one more thing to juggle for a little while and God's grace will enable me to do so. The grind of the Christian life can be full of discomfort, growing pains, and bothersome circumstances. If your ultimate pursuit is convenience, you have pledged allegiance to the wrong god.

MYTH #6: THE VISION STAYS THE SAME

We opened the book with an anecdote about a church that was crushed by a new pastor who came with a *completely* different vision from what existed. While this sort of dynamic can prove dangerous, this does *not* mean that the vision of the new leader is going to be a carbon copy duplicate of the former leader. There can and should be differences.

The new vision should *complement* the former vision rather than *copy* the former vision. Even in our case, I had come up in the church, yet the vision I feel God gave me was not an exact mirror of what existed. For example, the vision before was, "Making disciples who make a difference." Pastor Terry had emphasized this from the start. He is a teacher to the core and injects teaching into every conversation he has. Discipleship is as natural as breathing to him.

Where Pastor Terry is a teacher, I am more of an evangelist/preacher in my pastoral emphasis. While the end goal of making disciples stays the same, I've modified the vision slightly to "Reaching all people from all walks of life with the Gospel of the Kingdom to make disciples who make a difference." You'll notice that the beginning of the statement is the piece of my heart and vision that I brought to splice into the existing one. Why is that important? The people who were part of the church when Pastor Terry was leading were drawn to his teaching gift, and some have ultimately left because I am less of a teacher. Coupled with that ministry difference is a disparity in personality, as well. Pastor Terry is more introverted, preferring a small group of people he can teach to standing on a platform. I am much more outgoing; I enjoy the stage and have a habit of talking to everyone, everywhere.

Neither is good or bad; it›s just reality. Another example that comes to mind is John/Joel Osteen. John, who founded the church, was a fiery evangelist. When his son Joel took over, he, too, was an evangelist, but his personality was much more soft-spoken and nurturing. These differences can be a challenge for a congregation to adapt to. Nevertheless, it's important to note that things like vision, personality, and style may vary from one leader to the next, and that is okay. Don't buy into the myth that you, as a new leader, must be a copy/paste reproduction of the former leader. There is room for your unique God-given vision.

MYTH #7: TRANSITION IS A SPEEDY PROCESS

Had I known it would take this long, I would have never done it. It's something we have all found ourselves thinking or saying at some point. We tend to miscalculate the pace of big transitions in life. We underestimate the workload and overestimate our own adaptability. A better and more affordable apartment comes available for rent and you think it's nothing more than a simple move across town. Six months later, you're still unpacking boxes.

The truth is, dust can take a while to settle. When a big move of any kind takes place, you might have months of awkward adjustment as all parties settle in. Build this into your planning and your expectations. Humans are usually not quick-change artists. You cannot expect team members, spouses, congregants, or children to instantly adapt to a brand-new environment.

If you have never set a budget as a family, you can expect several meetings ahead to reallocate, to talk through best practices, and to keep yourselves accountable. New practices toward spending will not instantly feel like natural habits. They could take months to pin down.

The biggest transition anyone could ever go through is going from the kingdom of darkness to the kingdom of light through salvation in Christ Jesus. While the conversion is instant, the *working out* of this salvation will take a lifetime. The New Testament refers to us as "saved" and also refers to us as "being saved" (see Romans 5:1, 1 Corinthians 1:18). In other words, we have transitioned, yet we are constantly transitioning. It is an ongoing work, and our calling is to embrace it instead of trying to shortcut it.

Now, this does not mean it should take you ten years to settle into a new job. We still have to be practical about timelines. However, timelines can be deceptive. Don't be surprised if things take longer than you thought they would. When I was handed my role at the church, the actual hand-off was a single instant on the platform during a Sunday morning service. However, fleshing it out took months and many people besides myself had to walk through it. In some ways, the transition is still unfolding.

Big shifts rarely affect just one person. There are many lives touched by the winds of change. It can be messy, challenging, and full of twists and turns. Nevertheless, stay anchored to the original vision and see it through to completion. Don't stop the change before it has a chance to change! Reject the misconceptions and hold fast to the truth. While ignorance is awful, deception is worse yet. George Bernard Shaw said, "Beware of false knowledge; it is more dangerous than ignorance." When we are deceived, we are fully pursuaded of truth that is not truth. Many have made giant leaps based on bad information, misconceptions, and myths. As a result, they have paid an incredible price.

There are a number of stories out there about Christians who made giant transitions to remote and unreached places as missionaries without actually getting a word from God to become missionaries in the first place. In these cases, they based their leap on misinformation and zeal, and often die early or bear no fruit in the process. Misconceptions can cost us years of our lives and even our lives themselves.

John Maxwell said, "Disappointment is the gap between expectations and reality." If our expectations are misguided and we've bought into the myths, we set ourselves up for despair. Let me encourage you as you gear up for transition: reset your expectations and place them on Jesus. Leave the results to Him. After all, promotion does not come from the east, the west, the north, or the south (see Psalm 75:6). Promotion comes from the Lord. Often, this promotion comes in the form of a *plan* which acts as a lighthouse during those unpredictable times of change.

CHAPTER FIVE

THE PLAN

By Terry Moore

"If you fail to plan, you are planning to fail." — Benjamin Franklin

THERE IS A famous anecdote of a man who was shipwrecked and treading water in the ocean. He had been swimming in choppy waters and praying for some time when a boat showed up next to him. The fisherman on the boat threw him a circular lifebuoy and the man's response was surprising: "No thank you, brother. I'm waiting on the Lord."

As silly as this example might seem, many Christians fail to see the connection between the spiritual response from God and the practical means by which He answers prayer. If we neglect the spiritual side, practical results will suffer. If we don't value the practical side, we can miss the spiritual altogether. In other words, our lives as believers are in a constant state of tension. This is not a bad thing. In fact, it's what keeps us in a place of balance.

We maintain tensions between biblical truths all the time beyond examples like the "practical" and "spiritual." For example, we want to be tender, yet stern when needed. We want the blessings of God while also understanding we may suffer at times. We want to live generously, but we don't give to the point of not being able to feed our kids. Staying in balance requires regular maintenance.

One of our mentors, Dudley Hall, was teaching his daughter to drive. As they went along, he noticed that he was nearly hovering over the ditch on his side of the vehicle. Naturally, he called it out. Instead of getting back to the center of the lane, she whipped the wheel and ran into the ditch on the other side of the road. The Lord spoke to him at that moment. "That's about like you. The only time you're in balance is when you're going from one ditch to another."

Why do I bring up the concept of tension and balance? Because the process of transition is a tension between *sound planning* and *Spirit-led adventure*. Major transition is carried out in a tension between a proper, detailed schedule and the willingness to veer from the script when God says so. If a succession plan, for example, is too ordered and controlled, you will quench the Spirit. If it is too loose and free, you will create chaos. We want to enjoy the Spirit-led process of succession without ignoring God's lifebuoy called a written plan.

Having said that, the principles in this chapter are just that: *principles*. They are not laws set in stone that every succession plan must implement all the time. Instead, they are guiding truths that can be applied as needed to individuals and organizations. Consider them blueprints that can be used as a template and tweaked as needed for your specific case. After all, no transition is the same, which means there are no one-size-fits-all instruction manuals. My endeavor here is to provide some basic truths to get us thinking in the right direction.

THE KING'S DOMAIN

Your succession plan starts the moment you begin discipling people. You are building your plan when you start building people. This is true outside of the ministry, as well. The moment you begin training and delegating tasks in your business is the moment you are raising up possible successors. When Pastor Chris first visited Sojourn Church several decades ago, I wasn't aware that I was carrying out the most critical step in my eventual succession plan: raising up someone to come after me.

Whether you have been mindful of succession or not, God knows. When you begin to toss around the idea of handing over an organization, you will find that God has been making arrangements long before the topic hit your mind. This is the reality of the kingdom. You and I are participants in the kingdom, which means we are interconnected and all serving the singular purpose of expanding that kingdom on earth. Jesus only used the word "church" twice, yet He spoke of the *kingdom* over and over again. If someone mentions the word "church," you might just think of a building with a steeple. However, the kingdom brings to mind people, a system, a network, an economy, an entire divine ecosystem where God is ordering our steps before we even realize He is.

We know the word kingdom means "the king's domain," but has that become a cliché buzzword? I certainly hope not. Being in the King's domain means that we are plugged into God's economy, and we will find that He has provision, resources, guidance, people, deals, and strategies in place before we ever decided to plan a transition to begin with. One of the more famous passages in the Old Testament reads, "'For I know the *plans* I have for you,' declares the LORD, '*plans* to prosper you and not to harm you, *plans* to give you hope and a future'" (Jeremiah 29:11 NIV, emphasis added). *Plans, plans, and more plans!*

Three times the word *plan* is used here in a single verse. Plans precede prosperity. Plans facilitate our purpose. If God is a planner, and we are called to be like Him, we should be planners, as well. There are a few reasons why many ignore this, though, and lack a proper succession plan. Unpreparedness of this sort can wreak havoc on an organization.

MAPPING YOUR MONEY

As mentioned previously, there are giant pitfalls in holding on to a position for too long. It happens among pastors constantly. At times, it's due to pride or fear, but more often than not, it's money-related. If there is no money to retire on, they simply don't let go of their role. If a church has no money in the bank to pay a lump sum pension or to continue the salary for many years, the pastor may hold on far longer than he really should. Paychecks can be a sort of addiction that blinds us to the actual will of God in the matter. All of this is exacerbated by the fact that many ministers have opted out of social security, leaving them without a pre-arranged safety net when they hit retirement age.

I would advise that, as early as possible in the organization›s development, set up a retirement plan for senior staff members. This means the pastor needs to meet with an advisor regarding a personal savings plan into things like IRAs and 401Ks. This should be a no-brainer for any employee or business owner of any kind. On top of this, though, I would encourage churches to create their own retirement plan for senior leaders in addition to anything that leader might be stowing away personally.

There are a number of creative ways to tackle this issue. I'll list a few options in the bulleted list next. Just know, however, that the methods are not the most important thing. The timing is the most important thing. Start early! They say the best time to plant an apple tree is twenty years ago. The second best time is today. Jump on your money plans early and this will free up the church to experience a healthy, on-time succession.

- Create provision for a pension fund within the church's bylaws. The church payroll committee might add money (usually based on a percentage of salary) to the pension fund with each paycheck for a designated number of years. This can look like matching contributions or giving contributions regardless of employee input.
- Collect a love offering—or multiple love offerings. Dr. Lester Sumrall did not receive a regular paycheck from his church. Instead, he received an offering once annually which he lived on for the remainder of the year. This works if you have a church of decent size. These types of special legacy offerings can continue beyond the pastor's tenure or could be added to a pension fund in preparation for the hand-off of the organization.
- Agree to installments. Perhaps no savings are available and no preparations have been made. The church may still be able to agree to ongoing

pension payments that equate to a certain percentage of the pastor's salary. Include a clause that the pension payments are contingent upon future organizational income.
- Become an advocate. Job placement is not just for young students graduating college. There are many large churches that need experienced pastoral care on staff who would gladly hire a former founder to love on people. In this, a pastor can spend his golden years carrying out his calling, and receiving income, yet not carrying the same heavy load of leading an organization.

The details, bylaws, and logistics of this sort of financial maneuvering need to be worked out with professionals. I'm simply making the point that there are a number of ways that make it work. Get the board together and be proactive in setting aside funds and easing the financial burden of a leader when they hit retirement age. This will free up the church to slide into a new era without the threat of financial uncertainty.

We cannot overstate the importance of this type of planning. For very tiny churches of ten people, they likely cannot support a pastor's salary, so the pastor is usually bi-vocational and has his own retirement plan outside the church anyway. For very large churches, they can usually afford lump sum payments or ongoing pensions regardless of planning. For small to mid-size churches, though, this advice is particularly important to consider. Most churches in America have around seventy-five congregants.[8] This means for most pastors in the United States, the question of retirement and pension will require very careful planning and consideration.

Everything changes in ministry and business all the time. After decades in the grind, leaders can become ossified and refuse to adapt. When you wait too long and things decline, you set the successor up for failure and they often cannot recover. When money or other issues keep us in a position for too long, we step outside of the grace we need for the job. We begin to operate in the flesh and the results testify of that.

Eliminate your dependence on outside factors and remain dependent on Jesus. In this, you will be mobile and ready to spring into the air when God says jump. There are inverse problems with timing we should mention here also. Just as there are pastors and leaders who hold on for too long, there are those who let go too soon. In the same way that *money* causes pastors to overstay their welcome, *burnout* generally causes them to leave too soon.

LIVING BEYOND BURNOUT

According to a very recent Barna study, 46% of pastors admitted to considering quitting full-time ministry in the past year.[9] The reasons? They are carrying too much and they have not trained people to whom they can delegate authority. The study cites that pastors are overwhelmed by the stress of the job; they are lonely, isolated, and run ragged by the political climate.

At Sojourn, we created ways for all staff to go through personal ministry checkups. Not only do we have a third-party audit of our internals, books, and so forth, but we encourage our employees to engage with third-party counselors and consultants. We want them to maintain a personal love for God, for their families, and the ministry itself.

I am a firm believer in the fact that you need someone above you, someone under you, and someone beside you in the ministry. The person above you would be a spiritual father who has been where you are and has felt what you feel. Stay open to them; be accountable to them. It's been said that *accountability* and *visibility* go hand in hand. Schedule regular meetings for checkups on your soul.

You need someone under you. This would be a Timothy to your Paul. If you are not discipling people, you are not in the gospel ministry. Discipleship breeds a sense of purpose and adds a thrill to any calling. If no discipleship is happening, the pastoral role will quickly become dry.

Similar to Paul and Barnabas, you need someone to run *beside* you. They aren't necessarily a mentor and they aren't someone you are discipling, but someone who is on the same plane as you. It could be a fellow pastor across town who is in a similar season of life. These relationships provide at least one very valuable resource: *relatability*. Peter said, "The same sufferings are experienced by your brotherhood in the world" (1 Peter 5:9). You are not alone, and keeping a co-laborer by your side will remind you of that.

Quitting too soon has caused churches to collapse and families to fall apart. When the congregation is caught off guard and no viable successors are in place, the sheep scatter and things quickly go under. Framing up a game plan in these areas will keep you from premature *or* late transitions. Work to eliminate anything that would tempt you to dodge God's perfect timing. Knowing the risks and pitfalls will help you plan accordingly.

THE NITTY GRITTY

It could just be my personality, but I tend to feel that ten- and fifteen-year plans are overrated. I like to put one foot in front of the other and stay consistent above all else. Steadiness is in my personality, so I tend to favor this approach to building. In the early days of pioneering, people would ask me, "What's the vision!? What are you seeing!?"

My answer? *Make disciples, just like the Bible teaches.* The truth is, I did not have the next Sunday planned out, let alone some visionary apostolic takeover of a nation.

I knew that if we were going to get anywhere in the long run, it would require grinding it out day by day. This does not mean that we had *no* vision. It means we had a vision that was simple and workable.

My communication style on this front has always been somewhat casual. I tend to be less direct than some, which is something I picked up from my dad. I remember as a young boy, a friend and I were throwing rocks at each other outside. My dad came out with two guns and said, "Why don't you two go shoot each other? Cause I don't wanna take you to the hospital after a rock busts your head open." It was a funny and roundabout way of getting the point across: stop throwing rocks.

I am generally more roundabout and even-tempered with instructions and vision casting, as well. Make no mistake: visions and plans are wonderful, but they need to be *actionable*. For plans to work, they must contain practical steps that we can bring into practice *today*. I'm not against long-term planning, obviously, but the long-term plan should be touching the present in some way. For example, a retirement account is a long-term plan, yet it is actionable *today*. On the other hand, having some generic twenty-year plan to fly to the moon is not going to get you to the launch pad if you don't have actions you can take in the present.

James, the New Testament writer, corrected the hubris that many in the early church had with their big plans. He simply wrote, "You do not know what will happen tomorrow" (James 4:14). He corrected the arrogant projections and predictions that people were framing up for their lives without consideration for the Lord. At the same time, the Bible introduces yet another tension to us. In many passages, the Scriptures encourage wise planning for the future (see Luke 14:28-30, Proverbs 16:3, Psalm 20:4). Ultimately, we have a balance to maintain between focusing on the day that is in front of us and partnering with God to form wise plans. Solomon describes this balance well, writing, "There are many plans in a man's heart, nevertheless the Lord's counsel—that will stand" (Proverbs 19:21). In other words, we are free to plan wisely with the caveat that God can interrupt and modify those plans at any time.

Having said that, what should your transition plan look like? For starters, if it is not written, it doesn't exist. If you are changing jobs, you generally want to see a written offer or contract. If you are booking a flight, you write down or print confirmation numbers and trip details. Written words are *actionable* words. If it only exists in your head, you might struggle to get others on board. God knew this when He told Habbakuk, "Write the vision and make it plain on tablets, so that those who read it may run with it" (Habbakuk 2:2 PARA).

When God says to write the vision and make it plain, He is not telling us to use our best handwriting. He is telling us to be clear about the details of the plan. Without that, it cannot be implemented by others. Written plans keep us accountable. Black ink on white paper can settle disputes, ease tensions, and get us back to the center.

As we've navigated the transition at Sojourn, we've been helped immensely by the Gateway network. Gateway designates millions per year in their budget to help other churches. They have several full-time staff who exclusively work to assist other churches. As you can imagine, their waiting list is quite long. One of the major resources they provide is written material that acts as a blueprint for transitions, issues, internal systems, and administrative plans of all sorts.

If we call, they'll send us their bylaws, constitution, policy sheets, or transition outlines—no questions asked. When I mention the value of planning your transition, I am not suggesting you start from scratch. Instead, build from your network and pull on the resources of others. Learning from those who have walked where you are about to walk is a great way to future-proof your organization. In the remainder of the chapter, I want to discuss some additional elements to your transition that are worth considering, writing down, and implementing.

THE SCHEDULE

While our shift at Sojourn was abrupt, I do understand that many churches and businesses plan for a hand-off many years in advance. Timelines and schedules are critical to a transition plan. Consider carrying out the transition in phases, assigning dates and times and teams to each respective phase. One of the biggest frustrations for employees and volunteers is not necessarily being overworked or underappreciated. Often, it's failed expectations. When people are expecting a transition to take place in short order, yet there are no dates on the calendar or parameters set, and the transition is delayed for years on end, you are asking for trouble. They're being kept in the dark and their expectations are being let down. The same thing is true when transition is sprung on folks too quickly.

The truth is, people can usually handle fast or slow transitions. They can manage high workloads or light ones. They can navigate seasons of overtime and seasons of sabbatical. What they cannot manage very well, though, is being left in the dark and having no clue what to expect from one day to the next. Plan accordingly.

When a young couple gets engaged, what is one of the very first things they do? They open a calendar and set a date. Because they are serious about their commitment to each other, they put the wedding on the calendar and that date holds them accountable. Many people like the idea of succession, transition, job changes, selling a home, or going to college. The problem is, they don't open a calendar and give themselves dates and deadlines. Because of this, the idea remains an idea.

Build a schedule into your written plans. Transition can be inconvenient, which means it does not *conveniently* fit into your calendar. You have to carve out room for it. Part of the job of the schedule is to keep the pace of the transition in check. There are so many factors that play a part in the speed of transition. Things like age, burnout, energy levels, health, and the state of the organization all play a role. With a board or team of trusted advisors (see Proverbs 11:14), craft a written schedule that all relevant parties can agree to and run with.

OPERATIONS AND LOGISTICS

If your plan lacks administration, it is no plan at all. When Paul addressed the church at Corinth, he said, "And God has appointed these in the church: first apostles, second prophets, third teachers, after that miracles, then gifts of healings, helps, *administrations*, varieties of tongues" (1 Corinthians 12:28, emphasis added). Notice, Paul places administration in the same sentence as apostolic work and miracles. They are all valuable and necessary gifts from God.

Administration is more than shuffling papers and paying bills. The Greek word for administration in this passage is *kubernēsis*, which suggests *steering* or *piloting* within the affairs of the organization. Logistical operations are not *minor* roles but *guiding* roles that must be accounted for.

It cannot be overstated that a ministry involves and requires business operations. Budgeting, expense reporting, IT, and human resources can be overwhelming. While the senior leader is focused on ministry, it is imperative to have a good operations person(s) in place to take care of these practical things. Handing over operations from a previous team should be a slow, training process to ensure everything runs smoothly.

Before succession, this means verification of how operations will be handled before, during, and after the shift. The involvement of the new senior leader's role in operations also needs to be outlined. As tempting as it may be, a senior pastor will be best served by excusing himself from the day-to-day involvement in every aspect of the business side of ministry. A solid operations team will keep him privy to what's happening. This might mean a system of weekly, monthly, or quarterly reporting. Regardless of your path forward, don't neglect the role of administration in your plan. It is one of the components that can cause a transition to succeed or collapse.

CANDIDATE SELECTION

When I transitioned the church, the selection process was fairly straightforward and obvious. Of course, what's obvious to us is not always obvious to everyone else. One difficulty was the age disparity between incoming and outgoing leadership. Chris and I have a thirty-year age gap between us. As a leader, you can typically reach people within twenty years of your age. This meant that many of our older members were not as comfortable with someone much younger than them leading. On the flip side, many who would not have preferred a mature pastor such as myself are drawn to Chris, who is closer to their age.

These types of concerns are to be expected, even in cases where the candidate might be obvious. Concerns can be amplified when the next leader is not such an obvious choice. I understand that an obvious candidate is not a luxury that every organization has. With churches, non-profits, and businesses, the person to take the organization into a new era may not always be so clear. Often there is a sense of competition where candidates are jockeying and vying for position. Shoulders are climbed and politics run rampant. This should not be so in Christ-centered environments.

We curtail this drama through a path of humility and submission. This does not mean everyone will be happy with the outcomes. Joseph's brothers certainly were not happy that their father showed favor toward him. They sold him into slavery as payback! Things like jealousy and entitlement can rear their ugly heads when reins are being passed. Elijah did not allow his troubles with false prophets and unrepentant people to keep him from handing over his mantle to Elisha. Work through these road bumps and keep your eyes on the goal. There are a number of obvious questions to ask when choosing the next leader. For instance:

- Does this person get our organization's culture?
- Will this candidate's weaknesses be detrimental to our goals?
- What problems are coming for our industry and can this person solve them?
- Does this individual embody our vision?
- What have previous subordinates said about this leader?

The list goes on. There are a million good questions that could be asked when picking an employee. However, major succession is not merely the hiring of an employee. It is entrusting something precious and valuable to someone who could either make it or break it.

The flagship story of candidate selection in Scripture, which we can draw great insight from, is the story of Samuel anointing David. David had a number of brothers who all seemed like good options. They stood before Samuel consecrated and ready to be picked. When Samuel saw the firstborn, Eliab, he thought he would be the obvious choice. Instead, God said, "Do not consider his appearance or his height, for I have rejected him. The Lord does not look at the things people look at. People look at the outward appearance, but the Lord looks at the heart" (1 Samuel 16:7 NIV). After examining all of the brothers, Samuel did not see God's hand on any of them for the role. Reluctant, Jesse then mentioned that his youngest boy, David, was out in the field tending to sheep. Of course, we know that David was the man. It's important to note, though, that David was not necessarily the perfect pick according to man, yet he was the perfect pick according to God.

Many times, pioneers look to replace themselves with a younger version of themselves. This is not always a good idea. Instead, look to where the organization is going, look around at the new and unique environments, and see who God is raising up to meet the challenge head-on. When we pick people merely because they resemble a younger version of ourselves or because of outward appearance, it is like choosing Eliab instead of David. In the short run, it might seem right, but in the long run, it will cost everyone dearly. Stick with the will of God in the matter and you cannot go wrong.

Ideally, you have time to see the candidates perform under pressure and to see their integrity shine. This may come from direct observation or from referrals when hiring. Good character is the bare minimum requirement. Whether you're handing over a donut shop or a Fortune 500 company, you want to ensure that the successor is without compromise. There's a famous story of a businessman who was growing old and knew it was time to choose a successor to take over the business. Instead of choosing one of his directors or his own kids, he decided to do something different. He called all the young executives in his company together.

He said, "It's time for me to step down and choose the next CEO. I have decided to choose one of you." They were shocked. He continued, "I am going to give each one of you a seed today—a very special seed. I want you to plant the seed, water it, and come back here a year from today with what you have grown from the seed I've given you. I will then judge the plants that you bring, and the one I choose will be the next CEO."

One man, named Jim, was there that day and he, like the others, received a seed. He went home thrilled and told his wife the story. She helped him get a pot, soil, and compost, and he planted the seed. Every day, he would water it, give it sunlight, and watch to see if it had grown. After about three weeks, some of the other executives began to talk about their seeds and the plants that were sprouting. Jim kept checking his seed, but nothing ever grew.

Three weeks, four weeks, five weeks went by, and still nothing.

By now, others were talking about their plants, but Jim had nothing and felt like a failure. Six months went by—still nothing in Jim's pot. He figured he had somehow killed his seed. Everyone else had trees and tall plants, but he had nothing. Jim didn't say anything to his colleagues, however. He just kept watering and fertilizing the soil.

A year finally went by and all the young executives of the company brought their plants to the CEO for inspection. Jim told his wife that he wasn't going to take an empty pot, but she encouraged him to be honest about what happened. He felt sick to his stomach. This was, no doubt, going to be humiliating. With an empty pot in hand, Jim arrived to see tall varieties of plants grown by the other executives, and a few colleagues had a laugh at Jim's empty pot.

When the CEO arrived, he surveyed the room and greeted the young executives. "Wow, what great plants, trees, and flowers you have grown," said the CEO. "Today one of you will be appointed my successor!" The CEO then spotted Jim at the back of the room with his empty pot. He ordered the Financial Director to bring him to the front. Jim was terrified.

When Jim got to the front, the CEO asked him what had happened to his seed and Jim told him the story. The CEO asked everyone to sit down except Jim. He looked at the nervous young man, and then announced to the other executives, "Behold your next Chief Executive Officer!"

Jim couldn't believe it. Hadn't he failed the assignment?

The others were stunned. Then the CEO said, "One year ago today, I gave everyone in this room a seed. I told you to take the seed, plant it, water it, and bring it back to me today. But I gave you all boiled seeds; they were dead and it was never possible for them to grow. All of you, except Jim, have brought me trees and plants and flowers. When you found that the seed would not grow, you substituted another seed for the one I gave you. Jim was the only one with the courage and honesty to bring me a pot with my seed in it. He followed instructions and valued honesty—instead of just trying to impress me. Therefore, he is the one who will be the new Chief Executive Officer!"

It goes without saying that *integrity*, at the end of the day, is the ingredient a successor cannot in *any way* lack.

LOOP IN STAFF

The impact a big transition will have on current staff is not a small issue to keep in the margins. It should be central to your plan and your communication channels. For example, in our case, at the time of the transition, the staff had been in relationship with Chris and anticipated a continued great working relationship. In hindsight, it would have been wise for me to talk with the senior team, informing them that the change might impact their current role and that I had no way of controlling the outcome.

With a regime change of any kind, guarantees from the former administration are no longer active and changes that might not have occurred prior are suddenly on the table. This is the natural flow of transition across any organization. It's important that staff are aware of the possibilities.

In our situation, one of the pastors on staff who had been asked if he would be considered for the role was suddenly out of consideration. This created some instability for him and his family, as they began to now report to someone who had once been a colleague. Having to now view a "brother" as the leader was not an easy transition to make. Expectations of roles should be addressed for all senior staff pre-transition, with a caveat that nothing is promised.

BREAK GLASS IN CASE OF EMERGENCY

All organizational bylaws need a "break glass in case of emergency" clause. Who takes over if the senior pastor dies? What occurs if there is a moral failure? What constitutes a moral failure? What if a top executive uses funds illegally?

Neither secular nor Christian entities are immune to scandal, foul play, and "suddenlies." It's critical to think about what to do in a crisis transition while there are no major crises to deal with. For churches and businesses alike, emergency succession plans are a necessary part of the plan. When emergencies arise, we already have a slew of emotions and pain to deal with. We don't want to have to go about consequential organizational planning in the midst of that. When churches fail to have an emergency plan together and something goes south, it's sort of like running around trying to find a first aid kit while the wounded person bleeds out. It's far better to have an easy-to-locate first-aid kit ready to roll.

This plan should include details on transfers of authority, money, delegation, communication channels, third-party input, and more. There have been churches that have had devastating moral failures among leadership, and without a proper emergency protocol and documentation in place, the organization caves. This sort of thing usually results in lawyers getting involved and boards scrambling to patch up the situation. In the same way that the President of the United States has multiple emergency successors (Vice President, then Speaker of the House), it's wise to name a first and second successor, if possible. *Or* create a voting system in which a qualified board can quickly bring in a successor. There are a number of templates for this sort of planning available online. The goal of this heading is to simply encourage you to get *something* in writing.

At the end of the day, God Himself is the initiator of a healthy transition. Whether it is seeking counsel through prayer or consulting with trusted spiritual leaders, recognizing and submitting to God's guidance is crucial in ensuring that you are in line with His will before, during, and after the transition occurs. We've discussed candidate selection and organizational hand-off in some general terms thus far, but in the following chapter, Pastor Chris will walk you through the unique edge we've found in our succession plan and how you can do the same.

CHAPTER SIX

THE FAMILY

By Chris McRae

"Train people well enough so they can leave, treat them well enough so they don't want to." —Richard Branson

IF YOU'VE BEEN hired at a handful of companies in your career, you've probably heard some version of, "We are sort of like a family around here." When hearing this, you might have felt reassured or maybe you saw red flags. After all, some managers say things like this in order to exploit a team's time or request big favors and unpaid overtime under the guise of familiarity. Others call themselves family as a form of denial, covering up a toxic work culture. There are countless articles that cite the dangers of slapping the label "family" on anything an organization does. At the same time, the core of the "family" message is a very, very good one if applied correctly. Families fight for one another, help one another, and desire the best for all its members. Families applaud each other, forgive one another, and carry a sense that they are a part of something bigger than themselves.

Being a family, as an organization, means the individual members are not just numbers on a spreadsheet or cogs in a system. They are appreciated, loved, and valued members of the unit. This is particularly true when it comes to working in the house of God. When a co-worker is not just a colleague, but a brother or sister in Christ, the investment in the relationship becomes more intentional. You begin to care about the person's soul just as much as you care about their output. You aren't just overseeing their production—you're shepherding their hearts.

The commitment level to the relationship is simply higher when organizations implement the family model in a healthy way. I've seen this firsthand in my time at Sojourn while working under Pastor Terry. If we had a cold, corporate approach to ministry, I would clock out at the end of the day, say farewell, then see my boss and co-workers again at the next shift. This wasn't the case. Well beyond normal work hours, gatherings, functions, and hunting trips kept us interconnected. We did life together—and still do. Pastor Terry, for instance, does not particularly enjoy fishing. Yet he would take me fishing because he knew *I* loved it.

While we would cast our lines, he would pour into me and check up on me, and I would draw from his wisdom. These times for bonding and impartation were facilitated by the core value that we really are a family. This approach made all the difference when it came time for the church to undergo our succession.

HOMEGROWN

Major League teams like the Mariners, Blue Jays, and Yankees all bring their people up through the farm system. These single, double, and triple-A teams work to develop players who might eventually go on to the majors. The Red Sox had historically done the same thing. The problem came about when a recent general manager for the Sox sold all the prospects from the minor league teams in order to stack the current major league team. They won a World Series—which was great. The problem is, the next year, the team went from first to *worst* because after trades had settled, nobody was left in the feeder system.

They fired him shortly after.

Several years of talent was sacrificed because the possible greats who were coming up through the ranks had been eliminated. Bringing in outsiders might be a decent short-term solution, but often, nothing beats homegrown talent. The general manager had bought people for a quick payoff rather than *developing* people for long-term results.

In the corporate world, 72% of new hires are internal, meaning they come from *within* the company.[10] There are a bunch of reasons as to why this approach is favored. The big one is this: the employee knows the culture, the environment, and the workflow and has a heart for the company. There is usually a certain fidelity there when someone climbs the ranks. Having a "heart for the house" is critical. With the family model, having a love for the organization and its people comes naturally. As you pour into those around you, discipling them and investing over the course of years or decades, those recipients will take on the DNA of the organization. They won't just have a duty to the work but a love for the very act of serving.

Jesus said, "I am the good shepherd. The good shepherd lays down his life for the sheep. The hired hand is not the shepherd and does not own the sheep. So when he sees the wolf coming, he abandons the sheep and runs away. Then the wolf attacks the flock and scatters it. The man runs away because he is a hired hand and cares nothing for the sheep" (John 10:11-13 NIV).

What is Jesus doing here? He is highlighting the difference between the true shepherd with a heart for the house and an outsider with no actual investment in the people. Does this mean that when you hire from the outside, you will always wind up with a hired hand who runs from wolves? Absolutely not. It does mean, though, that there are advantages to in-house successors. Those include:

- Observability. When developing people in-house, you can spend years observing their strengths, weaknesses, and character.
- Familiarity. Insiders simply require a smaller learning curve and generally adapt to new roles within the same organization more quickly than those who are adapting to both a new role and a new organization.
- Marketability. In the church world, this might not be the best term to use, but the point is, when congregants, employees, and volunteers are familiar with an individual, the buy-in and support can happen much quicker. It's easier to present an insider as the next organizational leader whereas an outsider may require a "dating phase" where all parties involved are feeling out the new guy or gal.

A homegrown heart for the house often creates a faithfulness that is hard for an outsider to match. Without this faithfulness to the vision, it's easy to just leave when a better offer comes along. In this, the senior pastor is on a rotating loop like corporate CEOs.

Here is where I need to give you a massive caveat:

many churches, non-profits, and businesses have no choice but to hire from the outside, and there is *nothing* inherently wrong with that. The John 10 lesson on outsiders does not mean that hiring a new executive from across town is going to lead to the neglect of the people. Outsiders absolutely can be good shepherds who reject the "hired hand" mentality. In fact, within many denominations, pastors might stick around for a few years on average before being moved on to a new congregation. In these cultures, churn is normal. In other situations, a church might have gone through internal pain to the point that no one from the inside is in a position to lead. In those cases, a neutral third party might come in and offer fresh vision, perspective, and healing.

The last thing I want to do in promoting the family model is completely bash the idea of recruiting and outside hiring. However, I do see a biblical case to be made for raising up disciples in-house who then raise up more disciples, and so on. As members of the family of God, we want tight-knit connections with those near us to whom we can entrust our ministries. Elijah wasn't posting a job opening. He picked the guy (Elisha) whom he had been mentoring for years. Moses wasn't throwing advertisements on Craigslist when his job as a forerunner was wrapping up. He chose the man (Joshua) who had been sticking close to him and the house of God.

When Pastor Terry was moving toward transition, I leaned in as a candidate and made myself available in every way possible. I didn't want to separate myself from the executive team nor drum up some new, opposite vision for myself. The potential of the new role was not an opportunity for me to flex my leadership muscles or manifest my authority. It was simply an extension of the service I had already been carrying out. There was no sense of competition nor jockeying for power. Because our transition was so relational, I assumed we had less need for strategy. I've learned since then that strategy is always necessary. I realized that Pastor Terry is a strategic thinker, and one of the reasons the church was so successful was because he was always thinking at least a year in advance. He knew what was coming, where he felt God was directing the church, and was ever prayerful. We have the mentality that we don't get to choose our family. While we know that's true in terms of blood, it's also true in terms of the family of God. You might not like everything that goes on, you might have disagreements, but at the end of the day, God picked your family—you didn't.

This mental framework keeps a spirit of offense off of you. It keeps you pliable and full of grace and understanding. It helps you to maintain faithfulness through the process. Because of the family model, Pastor Terry and I had a unique arrangement where he stayed on as the founding pastor, primary advisor to me, and still oversees the missions and financial aspect of the church. He continues to co-teach with me on Wednesday nights.

Not only has this minimized some of the possible issues, it's been a net benefit for me and the congregation. For starters, Pastor Terry staying around has been a huge endorsement for me in my new role. Congregants not only trust him but trust who and what he approves.

Beyond that, succession is often a time when division creeps in. An abrupt hand-off where the senior pastor rides off into the sunset can be an opportunity for people who've toyed with the idea of leaving for some time to actually go through with it. Transition has a way of occupying so much leadership bandwidth that folks can fall through the cracks and feel forgotten. With Pastor Terry staying around, it's been far less of a shock to everyone involved. Because we see one another as family, we are not caught up in competition or pride with one another. Not once have I felt any sort of power struggle, which is a testament to the reality that neither of us view the church as our own. It is and always will belong to Jesus. We are simply stewards.

Now, we are not naive on this point. It's fully understood that in most cases, keeping a former leader around is not going to be ideal or realistic. Usually it's absolutely best for the former to *not* stick around. Perhaps that person doesn't even *want* to stay. This does not negate the concept of the family model, though. It simply means that after raising up leaders to take your place, there is a time to step back and let them be with no input or on-site presence. Next, we will walk through some of the post-succession pitfalls to consider *if* the former leader plans to stick around, whether that looks like regular attendance in services or even general apostolic oversight.

MEDDLING

Whether it's in-laws taking over your wedding or a bureaucracy making it difficult to run your business—when people meddle, things get messy. Nobody wants to be treated like a child, but when we insert ourselves into the workflow of a new leader in an unwelcomed or controlling way, we are doing just that. When children are young, we are very direct as parents. "Don't do that. Go here. Say this. Quit touching that." Often, a child's life depends on our directness. As they get older, the directness is replaced with dialogue. Instead of having to yank their hands away from a hot stove, we are having meaningful conversations about the best path forward. As parents, we give our kids rope and allow them to step out, try, and sometimes fail. Some things invite our comments and other things do not. It's the nature of parenting children who are on the brink of adulthood.

These same realities exist in the church family. New disciples require lots of cleanup. They can be messy and will need to be told the same things many times over. As maturity happens, there is more liberty given. From that place, a less direct approach is warranted. By the time an organization is handed over, there should be a level of maturity and trust established that little direct, day-to-day feedback is required. In fact, there is an inherent distrust we are conveying when we question decisions, push back, or raise our eyebrows at every move the new leader makes. While I welcome and appreciate his feedback of any kind, Pastor Terry never makes me feel like I'm being crowded or like I'm under a microscope. Of course, if he saw me running for a cliff, he would throw a stick in front of my leg to trip me before jumping off. However, he is hands-off and gives me lots of wiggle room to call shots.

Let's say you have handed over an organization *and* you are sticking around. How do you gauge the amount of input that's appropriate to give? First off, I would say the default position should be that of a silent spectator. If it's January 1st and you are already prepping your vision for the year to bring to the team meeting—you haven't handed over the organization. You've just rebranded your tenure.

Make the decision to be an *observer* and a prayerful supporter from the start. From there, the new leader will pull on you as needed. With Pastor Terry, I have continually welcomed his feedback, correction, insight, and foresight. Not once have I felt he was meddling or attempting to pull levers behind the scenes. It simply is not in his DNA to meddle. We've also been very open with one another about expectations and our hearts for the house. This sort of dynamic only works if there is an open dialogue with clear expectations and a certain level of universal maturity.

WE NEVER DID IT THIS WAY BEFORE

There is another reason why the former leader should assume the role of a prayerful supporter, and it has little to do with the new leader and more to do with the congregation. When new decisions are made, the congregation or employee base will look to the former leader for their approval. Great difficulty can arise in these situations. When many in the congregation naturally still look to the former leader, it can cause unrest for the new senior pastor. The new leader may feel conflicted between trying to lead the way he feels God is calling him and trying to please the congregation and original pastor. Establishing the same respect as the founding pastor can be a challenge when the former leader sticks around. This might manifest as an abundance of questions or skepticism from those you are leading. You might hear comments like, "Well, we never did this before. The former leader told us otherwise. So-and-so tried this and it didn't work... why will it work now?"

If the former leader is expressing disapproval, shaking his head, and shrugging his shoulders from the sidelines, the faithful congregation will assume the demeanor of that leader and make life difficult for the new guy. The answer to "we have never done it this way before" is often "because we've never been here before."

Change is baked into the life cycle of any entity. Thank God that Paul wrote letters from a jail cell to the church. This doesn't mean that the church is bound to receive sermons from a jailed pastor *exclusively*. As circumstances change, so do the methods. It is up to the new leader and the former leader to communicate these things effectively. It's critical that the founding pastor and the new pastor are a united front. Parents might not agree on every detail of parenting, but they still present themselves as a unified force to the children. Why? Because they are serving a vision that's bigger than themselves and bigger than small disagreements. Congregants, employees, and children alike will crumble under the weight of mixed signals. Former and current leaders working together must rally around the core vision and present it accordingly.

The fact is, there are a million different types of leaders. I have had good old boy coaches that were kind and I've had some who could scare the daylights out of you. No matter the style, when they had the right heart, you knew they only wanted what was best for their players. The heart of the family is to ultimately benefit the family. This has continually been a guiding force in our own succession plan. Too often, we limit our thinking and do what "seems right" during a transition. The problem is that the Bible says, "There is a way that *seems* right to a man, but its end is the way of death" (Proverbs 14:12, emphasis added).

For instance, it might *seem* right to hire the most credentialed and well-educated outsider to take over. But what about the guy who knows the business like the back of his hand and has labored faithfully in-house for a decade? It might *seem* right to accept a huge job offer out of state, but what if that company is on the brink of bankruptcy? It might *seem* right to have a relative stay with you for six months, but what if it costs you the peace in your home?

This is why latching hold of the will of God cannot be understated. Have a heart that longs to *figure out* and *carry out* the will of the Father. This is the difference between the way that *seems* right and the way that *is* right. It would have been easy for Pastor Terry and his own son to organize a succession of the church. The truth is, his son didn't want the position, and God uses him in a different way to advance His kingdom. Pastor Terry was interested in the will of God in everyone's life, above a traditional father-son hand-off.

In the family model of discipleship, spiritual sonship can be as consequential as biological sonship. In fact, there are small churches everywhere limping along with a father-son succession plan forever. Because they have a paid-off building and an existing 501c3 structure, they keep the operation going without community impact or organic discipleship. Sometimes the best and most God-honoring succession plan is to close doors and join another entity as a prayerful participant in what God is doing.

FAMILIARITY

There is a final pitfall in the family model that we should be aware of. Jesus alluded to it when He said, "A prophet is not without honor except in his own country, among his own relatives, and in his own house" (Mark 6:4). Familiarity can hinder a person's ability to receive. When we do life with our church family, many of our shortcomings and issues are out there for them to see. You might do a fishing trip with men from the church, and on that trip, they might see you as a buddy rather than a pastor. Perhaps you watch the big game with a group from the congregation and you're just another member of the social circle for that evening. When we do life like this, it's a wonderful blessing. The risk to consider is that people might struggle when you have to put the "pastor" hat back on.

The congregation has to be flexible in this way. It's important they realize that, *yes,* you are the everyday man who was catching trout with them last week, but also, you are in a God-ordained position to instruct their lives from the pulpit with teaching, correction, insight, and wisdom that carries a big weight. There is a notorious struggle for the children of pastors to receive from their parents as pastors. A teenager might disregard a teaching on patience that their dad is sharing from the pulpit because, after all, that same dad was yelling at someone in traffic earlier in the week. With family comes familiarity, and with familiarity comes the temptation to not honor the gift and the office that God has given that person.

The same thing can happen in the corporate world. After a day of eating hotdogs at the company picnic with the CEO, it can be difficult to receive correction on Monday morning over a work issue. From the top down, honor must remain throughout the church or business. Despite doing life together and growing in familiarity, hard lines must be drawn and positions have to be honored. Let familiarity breed open dialogue and healthy communication. Don't let it breed dishonor and blurred lines.

BEYOND YOURSELF

We tend to think of transition as a one-person event. If Bill changes jobs, we ask Bill how his new job is going. However, the family can feel the weight of the change just as much as the individual with the new career. We need to ask ourselves, who else is attached to this move? Who is directly impacted and who is *indirectly* impacted? It's a myth to assume that transitions are isolated to an individual.

Big changes send shockwaves through families and communities. The aftershock can be felt by those we least expect. As I moved into the senior pastor position, my wife Vanessa was also stepping into new territory. As a natural introvert, being in the shadows was easy for her, but being the wife of the senior pastor was a sort of limelight that required an adjustment period. She was incredibly excited for me, but sending an introvert into a more public position can take its toll.

Here's a practical step you can take to shore up the transition for those around you. Before the big change, make a list of everyone that the change might impact. Don't leave anyone out. This list should contain people who are impacted in big ways and small ways. They might be impacted emotionally, physically, financially, or spiritually. From there, write out a quick game plan for communication. What needs to be communicated to these various parties and *how* does it need to be communicated?

For instance, some people can be addressed as a group. If there is a pastoral change, for example, you obviously won't be meeting one-on-one with every single congregant individually. These things can be discussed corporately. With others, like your spouse and children, the change will need to be talked about individually on an ongoing basis. You will want to provide ample support and ask the right questions. Those might include:

- How do you feel about this shift?
- What are the pitfalls of a transition like this?

- What will you need from me while we make this change?
- What is the end goal of all this and how can we get there together?
- What can I be praying for as we go about transition?

You cannot over-communicate during these critical times. Stay engaged with those around you through an open, judgment-free atmosphere of communication. Job changes are becoming more and more frequent in corporate America, which means families are routinely moving to new cities with new houses, churches, and communities to become comfortable with. This type of transition can be heavy on your children. Acknowledge their concern, fears, excitement, and hesitation. Take practical steps to ease the difficulty of the move. Work to cultivate a safe environment in the home. Life is not always steady for children, but dad and mom *can* be that much-needed, steady force for good.

This sort of mindfulness and open dialogue creates a groundwork in preparation for the transition. This groundwork will be of great use in allowing the whole move to work like a well-oiled machine. These principles not only apply within families but to employees, as well. Leaders should build bridges of communication between the new leadership and the support staff. When a leader comes or goes, their assistant usually does, too.

Support staff at every level can be left in the wake of the change, and they deserve clear communication as much as anyone. Build a space for concerns to be shared and questions to be asked. This will curtail hurt feelings and will limit growing pains.

When change happens to you, it happens to those closest to you, as well. The indirect consequences of a transition can be seen over the course of many years. Become an intentional communicator with a plan to show your support, ask the right questions, and create a functional shift. Families and organizations of all kinds have been bogged down with dysfunction for too long—your intentionality can change that.

CHAPTER SEVEN

THE ADJUSTMENT

By Terry Moore

"Often when you think you're at the end of something, you're at the beginning of something else." —Fred Rogers

NOW WHAT? IT'S a short, two-word question that anyone on the other side of transition finds themselves asking. I know I certainly did in January of 2020 when I had stepped out of my senior role. Fortunately, God has His ear inclined to the phrase "now what?" and was quick to give an answer. In fact, God has an answer to what's next before the current season ever closes.

Let me be clear, *retirement* is not a biblical term. One person said, "I can't retire because I never had a job to begin with. It was a calling." I tend to agree: our purpose continues until the day we leave the planet, and retirement is just not something I really ever consider. I have no issue with the word retirement, nor do I think the concept is wrong. We are not going to be occupying the same role and producing the same output at age eighty that we did at age thirty. What *is* wrong is the idea that the end of our normal working life is the end of our purpose and assignment in the kingdom. Retirement is not an excuse to be idle or unfruitful in the kingdom.

So, for the sake of simplicity, I may use the term "retirement" or "retirement age" in this chapter. I'm simply describing the golden era of life where our calling and emphasis have shifted. It's not a time to do nothing, sitting around, waiting for the sweet by and by. It is a new era of purpose and fulfillment. God can do more in your golden years than He did in the prior decades. Let's start thinking accordingly.

What do Geico, Coca-Cola, Home Depot, and McDonald's all have in common? They were started by founders who were over the age of fifty. Colonel Harland Sanders started his first Kentucky Fried Chicken restaurant at age sixty-five. Nine years and 600 franchises later, he sold it for millions. At the same age of sixty-five, Laura Ingalls Wilder began writing *The Little House on the Prairie*. Yuichiro Miura climbed Mount Everest at eighty and Harriette Thompson ran a marathon at ninety-one. In the faith world, Smith Wigglesworth was nearly fifty before he launched the ministry many know today. Bob

Pierce founded Samaritan's Purse at fifty-six and Lester Sumrall launched Feed the Hungry at age seventy-four.

It's not too late. Purpose does not fade but *flourishes* as we age. A change in assignment does not mean the end of an assignment. For the most part, people understand that retirement age is not a time to sit around and do nothing. In fact, nearly 50% of retirees follow a nontraditional retirement path that involves partial retirement, and at least 26% of retirees later unretire and return to some sort of work.[11]

It's important to know from the start that transition and handing off an organization is a promotion. It's not a downgrade and it's not even a horizontal shift. It's an upgrade! God does *not* take us from fulfillment to emptiness. Why? Because God takes us from glory to glory and strength to strength (see 2 Corinthians 3:18, Psalm 84:7).

It has been easier than some might expect for me to release the reins of the church. Why? It is easier to release reins when you know you have new ones to grab onto. Pastor Chris discussed the implications of the former leader sticking around in chapter six, but I do want to emphasize the need for letting go of the reins, should you stay. The new senior pastor has inherited something that is already functioning. The only way this works is for the founding pastor to walk in humility daily, by allowing the new leader to spread his wings, try new things, and walk out their leadership.

In some ways, the new senior leader could feel like the founder is always a shadow, watching everything he does. As a result, the new leader must be confident in who he is in Christ so that he is not intimidated by the founder's involvement. My heart›s desire is to father people and to help them become successful. This is especially true of a spiritual son. There is no competition between Chris and me, and the unique arrangement has worked. However, if we do not have a good answer to the "Now what?" question, we will be tempted to resume the authority we had before and meddle in the process. Rest assured, when you let go of the reins that God gave you, new ones are on their way.

AFTERGLOW AND CELEBRATION

I highly recommend anyone read J. Robert Clinton's book, *The Making of a Leader*. In it, he describes life in six distinct phases, which I believe we can all glean from. The final phase we will run with and build on in this chapter. Keep in mind, leadership might mean pastoring a church or it could mean raising children. Don't limit the application of these concepts by a preconceived, limited definition of the word *leader*.

With that in mind, any given Christian life tends to follow a trajectory as follows when it comes to leadership:

1. Sovereign Foundations. This is where a leader starts to become aware of his or her calling to leadership. It is a time when character is developing, skills are coming together, and one's calling is being wrestled with. There is a deep sense of God's calling and purpose, and the building blocks for the emerging leader's life are starting to lay the foundations for a life of leadership. This phase makes up our early experiences of dabbling in places of authority, yet we tend to have very little control and many things are decided for us. It is a sort of leadership infancy.

2. Inner Life Growth. This is a season where the leader is getting the hang of hearing and obeying God's leading. Consider this the spiritual garden where growth is happening and intimacy with God is developed. Fundamental encounters with Jesus may happen here which shape the rest of your life. Here the leader is often put through several major tests. Will you obey and submit wholeheartedly to God or take the easy route? Anyone who has built anything of value in Christian leadership knows that there is no shortcut to this season.

3. Ministry Maturing. In this stage, the leader is discovering and practicing their spiritual gifts. Both positive and negative lessons are being learned during this phase. Questions are being answered like: What are my strengths? What are my weaknesses? What gifts can I offer? Oftentimes there is a strong pull to get more training during this time to minimize one's weaknesses and

bolster one›s strengths. In the first three phases, God is primarily working «in» the leader, *not* through him. As Clinton articulates, "Many emerging leaders don›t recognize this, and become frustrated. They are constantly evaluating productivity and activities, while God is quietly evaluating their leadership potential. He wants to teach us that we minister out of what we are."

4. Life Maturing. Now we are transitioning from *reaching in* to *reaching out*. This is the phase where we export the good things that God has imported into us. Here the leader is using their spiritual gifts in a satisfying way. You gain a sense of priority and you learn where to best sow seed and invest time. You've learned how to respond to negative experiences in a godly manner. A mature fruitfulness comes about in this phase. Isolation, crisis, pain, and conflict take on a new meaning. "Ministry flows out of being" has new significance as the leader's character mellows and matures. The work of the ministry is not just about "doing" but "being." This means communion and intimacy with God become immensely more important than one›s "success" in ministry.

5. Convergence. This is the sweet spot. Here God takes the leader and places him or her in a role that matches the gift mix and experience so that ministry is maximized. Life maturing and ministry maturing peak together during this phase. Sadly, many leaders never get to experience this. Whether it's premature death or sin issues, leaders sometimes miss this convergence al-

together. For those who experience convergence, it is a time of transitional leadership where the baton is passed down to other faithful leaders who will continue to develop the leader's vision for the church or organization they have built.

6. Afterglow. The afterglow or "celebration," as Clinton describes it, is a stage where the fruit of a lifetime of ministry growth culminates in an era of recognition and indirect influence at broad levels. Leaders in afterglow have built up a lifetime of relationships and continue to exert influence in these relationships. People will seek out a leader who is in afterglow because of their consistent track record of remaining faithful to God and their calling. Their storehouse of wisdom gathered over a lifetime of leadership will continue to bless and benefit many.

Think of your legacy like an account where people will be able to approach and make withdrawals, even long after you're gone. By the time you are in afterglow, this account is set up and *being* set up. I believe it was Myles Munroe who said, "The world is run by dead men. Why? Because those dead men wrote books." In other words, we are continually being influenced and inspired by the legacies of people who have long passed. The work of our lives will impact people without us being aware of it.

This may be a time where you ask yourself, "Did I do enough? Was my impact what it could have been?

Did I maximize my gifts for the glory of God?" Often, we have a skewed view of our own impact. We fail to see just how big of a mark we made. For instance, in the business world, we know that customers are far more likely to leave a negative review after a bad experience than a positive review after a good one. Not only that, but people who have bad experiences with a business tell more people about it than if they had a good one.[12]

What does this mean for us? It means you have probably had a deep impact on someone's life, yet you never heard any feedback on the matter. Maybe a marriage was saved by a word you shared in a sermon, without you knowing it. Perhaps a young person changed the course of their life because of the example they saw in you, but you were unaware. It's possible that conversations have been had about how impactful your witness has been through the years, and you will never be privy to the content of those conversations. We are not aware of every compliment and praise report—and that's a good thing. Just know that your legacy will preach on your behalf regardless of how active you are in this afterglow.

For me, I've been occupying much time leading membership classes and working at putting together manuals, books, workbooks, and recordings of all of my teachings from years past. It is a compilation of my legacy that has been both rewarding and nostalgic as I look back through the years and compile what God has given me. In a way, I am experiencing the heights of my purpose because I am consolidating and formalizing all of the purpose I have been carrying out over the decades. I'm not saying this is the absolute surefire blueprint for how every pastor or leader should be handling their latter years. I am saying, however, that there is something special about making your life's work accessible through print and various media.

In the Scriptures, we see numerous examples of individuals going through times of transition and discovering a new purpose on the other side. Joseph was sold into slavery and later became a trusted advisor to Pharaoh. Ruth left her homeland and found purpose in serving her mother-in-law and ultimately becoming part of the lineage of Jesus. The disciples left their former lives as mostly blue-collar workers to follow Jesus and were given a new purpose in spreading the gospel. God has an answer to your "Now what?" before you ever ask the question. Lean in and walk it out.

REGRET

If you've seen the movie *Schindler's List*, you know what a hero Oskar Schindler was. He was a Christian businessman in Germany who saved the lives of over a thousand Jewish refugees during the Holocaust. He employed them in his factories, providing them with protection from the Nazis and preventing their deportation to concentration camps. He spent millions in modern currency to protect people. His courageous and humanitarian efforts are still praised to this day.

At the end of the movie, Schindler is close to being arrested by Nazis as a criminal and is about to make his escape. The workers he saved gather around him and he receives a letter signed by them in case he is caught. Stern, a co-laborer of his in the rescues, presents him with a gold ring, which has an inscription from the Talmud: "Whoever saves one life saves the world entire."

It's then that he looks at the ring, looks at his car, and even pulls a pin off of his suit coat and laments that he could have saved more. "Why did I keep the car?" he says, as he breaks down with regret. His workers surround him with support and embrace as the movie ends. Both his workers and those who watch the movie are all thinking the same thing: *Don't beat yourself up. You did so much!* Yet to him, he could not look past what he *could* have done.

While we can all understand his sense of regret, we should also know that this is no place to stay. Your afterglow should not be full of woulda-coulda-shouldas. Regret is grief over what cannot be changed. Grieving over the fact that you cannot change the past will only set you up for a sorrowful future. We are only liable to be hurt by our past when we still find our identity in it. The truth is, there are many people who are addicted to ministry and they get their worth from their work. When that work is no longer there, they feel they are less than some former version of themselves. If you wallow in regret over what you *could* have done, remember that your ultimate sense of identity is not found in *what* you do or what you *don't* do. It is found in the One who purchased your soul. Your identity is rooted in Christ, not your ministry output. Your position at the throne of God will always matter more than your position in the C-suite of a company.

Your purpose is less about the way you minister to people and more about the way you minister to the Lord. Your connection with Him comes before anything that may or may not be happening in the course of your career—ministry or otherwise. Your fulfillment does not dry up in the afterglow but should well up with a new sense of meaning and value.

The Bible is not a story of human achievement. It's not the glorification of what man can do, but what *God* can do. It is a document that exemplifies the overcoming, overpowering, and overwhelming goodness of God *within* the story of humanity. This whole thing is bigger than your own sense of accomplishment and achievement. Regret wants you to pay for your past with the currency of your present joy. Flee from this temptation and remember the words of Paul: "By the grace of God, I am what I am" (see 1 Corinthians 15:10).

There is an exciting time of fulfillment and activity waiting for you on the other side of your "Now what?" Don't occupy this time with inactivity or with regret. Instead, partner with Jesus as a co-laborer to see His will continue to manifest on the earth. It might look different than what you're accustomed to—and that's okay. Hold fast to the promises of God. Even in a mature age, learn to embrace the growing pains. There's still purpose in the process and glory in the grind!

THE PACE OF ADJUSTMENT

In the same way that Chris and Vanessa had their own unique path in adjusting to the change, Susan and I did, as well. My wife experienced a sense of loss that she simply had not anticipated. She had been the Senior Pastor's wife for over thirty years. She does not enjoy change. In fact, she never moves the furniture in our home once she likes where it is placed. With that position came a certain influence and responsibility. She was fine that the shift occurred. However, changing positions from being one of the key leaders into a more subtle role was new and took some adjustment.

She had poured just as much of herself into the ministry as I had through the years, and there was certainly a season of mourning that came with the transition. While the change might be abrupt, the adjustment can take time. There's nothing wrong with that. In hindsight, I could have been stronger with communication. When I felt God leading us to this transition, our oversight said *yes,* our elders said *yes,* and Susan said *yes.* As a result, I jumped into it. Looking back, having a unanimous *yes* does not mean that we bypass ample communication—even with those who seem like third, fourth, or fifth parties.

The adjustment was not only felt by me but by Susan and the rest of the family, as well. For instance, our kids and grandkids would often sit in the front row with us for the services. They grew up doing that. The grandchildren especially enjoyed this. They certainly still can sit with us on the front row—it just feels different to them when all of a sudden, Dad/Granddaddy isn't the pastor anymore. My family loves Chris and had no qualms about him assuming the Senior Pastor role, but the point is, the change was felt by those beyond spouses and family. For example, there were many staff members who had served for decades, who were experiencing a complete role shift, as well. This could not have been anticipated but should have been better prepared for by me and Pastor Chris. I recommend a transition plan be written out for all of the key personnel, particularly those who have served for a substantial length of time. On one hand, the assumption they remain in their current role is short-sighted, but so is assuming they will be forced to resign.

People truly are tied to their senior pastor. Congregants realize, *Hey, this is the guy who baptized my kids, vis-*

ited me in the hospital, and counseled us when our marriage was on the rocks. When this key individual no longer occupies the same role, it does send a ripple effect through the lives of many. When Moses passed away, the people did not think to themselves, *Oh, that guy is old news anyway.* No, in fact, they mourned and wept over him for a month (see Deuteronomy 34:8). Don't feel guilty over this. It is all in God's timing and perfect plan.

Because so many people are tied to the founding pastor, it's not a bad idea to consider shifting top-level leaders, oversight, or elder boards, as well, when a transition occurs. In the same way that a new president picks his cabinet, new pastors may want to be able to have some say-so in their elders and oversight. Again, this may change from one church government to the next. Regardless, in any case where a church is run by elders or a board, it is important to develop relationships between them and the incoming senior pastor. This requires time and effort to connect to and understand each other. The importance of this cannot be overlooked, though.

SUPPORTIVE OBSERVER

It has been said that there is no victory without sacrifice. If your retirement era is going to be victorious, you have to ask yourself, what is being given up? What is on the altar? I personally could not do what I am doing for the church now if I had not given up my spot as senior leader. The sacrifice of the former role has made room for increase. Perhaps your next steps won't look like mine. There are many retired pastors who have been hired into positions (volunteer or staff) to love on people at local churches and handle pastor care like funerals, weddings, visits, and so forth. There are folks in afterglow who've been able to consult, advise, and join boards to pour out direction and insight they've gained over the years. Some have taken to writing or spending more time with family. There are a number of paths to pursue; the important thing is that you take one and maximize it.

Let God develop a unique plan for you. In the ministry, I was always of the opinion that if you were just going to do what everyone else was doing, you might as well close your doors and go join the church down the street. The same thing is true in many other areas of life. You don't have to follow the Reader's Digest five-step plan for making the most of retirement. You can enjoy a faith-filled adventure hand-in-hand with Jesus as you finish the race set before you. This is about the kingdom, not our own pre-packaged retirement guidelines.

I have been delighted to watch the church ebb, flow, and adjust on the other side of this change. Chris has a different gift mix than me and I've enjoyed seeing him come into his own. He entered at a time of hot cultural debates. Mask or no mask? Vaccine or no vaccine? Do we have an in-person service or stream only? The traditional church was experiencing upheaval, and Chris was well-suited to handle the big decisions that were coming.

Chris has a very unique favor with people, and I've been overjoyed to see him catapulted into prominence in a more consequential position. He has had speaking engagements, podcast opportunities, and a measure of visibility that simply wasn't in my makeup. His evangelistic edge has brought a new wind to the church. Being able to celebrate what God is doing through him and his team has been foundational in my adjustment. If you cannot celebrate the new blessing in someone else's life, how can you handle your own?

Stepping back as a quiet observer has been a joy and a satisfaction in itself. I know one church where the senior pastor had stepped down but his wife did not. I recall being in one of their meetings, and it was clear within a minute of starting that she ran the show behind the scenes. This doesn't work for a host of reasons. Our afterglow is not a time to try pulling strings or moving pawns. It's a time to partner with the purposes of heaven to see to it that your latter days are even more invigorating than the former.

Your life's work can be tainted or preserved depending on how you manage this final sprint to the finish line. We have biblical heroes who fell short and others who finished strong. We would all do well to position ourselves the way Paul did, that is, to be able to say with confidence, "I have fought the good fight, I have finished the race, I have kept the faith. Now there is in store for me the crown of righteousness, which the Lord, the righteous Judge, will award to me on that day..." (2 Timothy 4:7-8).

CHAPTER EIGHT

THE AFTERMATH

By Chris McRae

"Change is not a threat, it's an opportunity. Survival is not the goal, transformative success is." —Seth Godin

THE PHRASE *HAPPILY ever after* might be a nice way to close a story, but it's an unrealistic expectation for life after a big change. Happily ever after comes with a price tag. Happily ever after takes maintenance and sweat. When big change happens, we can count on two things: collateral damage and collateral blessing. In the aftermath of transition, you are sure to find some much-welcomed surprises as well as unexpected problems. I'd like to present some pointers to you as you navigate your life after the change.

When the luster and shininess of a promotion wears off, we are left with work to steward. After the excitement fades and the congratulations are over, there is a job to be done, a task to be carried out, meetings to have, and people to care for. If we miss this and just rest on our laurels, we will defeat the purpose of the transition to begin with.

There are some who are addicted to transition. They love the excitement of an upgrade, an update, a promotion, or a move. Unable to sit still, they are changing jobs every three months and they have the moving company on speed dial. Many people grow discontent when it comes time to actually *do the work* that the transition led them to. Think of it like this: everyone wants to buy a boat until it comes time to maintain that boat. We all love the excitement of closing on a new home until it's 3 a.m. and there's a raccoon in the attic.

Just beyond the exciting change is the reality of that dirty four-letter word: *work*. The end of the transition is the beginning of the labor. Because I had watched Pastor Terry for years and had been deeply involved with the church staff, I had an idea of what my new day-to-day role might entail. However, nothing could fully prepare me for the weight of that office. You really don't know or understand the size of it until you open your arms and try to carry it. Whether you are becoming a boss, a new parent, moving cities, or getting married—the "honeymoon period" is usually short-lived. For a while, I felt like David in Saul's armor. There were growing pains and some clunkiness in my leadership to work through.

Ordination, commencements, and promotions are wonderful—but how do we navigate the challenges ahead? You might feel a sense of *completion* when you graduate college, but you're still at the starting line. The truth is, we won't see a checkered flag until Jesus calls us home. Until then, we've got to roll up our sleeves and put in the effort. While it can be tempting to bask in the glow of your new role, it's important to hit the ground running and start making progress.

What should that progress look like? It depends on several factors, but for now, I will speak based on my own experience as a successor. In this chapter, I'll also pass along several pieces of insight that were given to me as I made my transition.

1. VALIDATE EARNESTLY

A new person coming in should validate the experience of people who've been there. We mentioned in chapter two that one of the unique challenges of a successor is dealing with existing teams. One of the best ways to ease any tension or quell skepticism from an existing team is to validate their experience. Make it known to them that you are fully aware of their service, and that in moving ahead, you will value their take. When people spend years laboring in an organization and suddenly the leader changes, they want to know that their loyalty will not go to waste. They want to be reassured that they can still be heard and that they still have a seat at the table.

What does this look like practically? Good old meetings—and lots of them. Some formal, some informal. It doesn't have to be an official board room sit down with an agenda and catered lunch. It might just be a quick conversation in passing. Regardless, the value of intentional connection needs to be noted here. There are new pastors who make it a point to visit with every family in the church. One seasoned minister went on about 500 visits a year in order to connect with his congregation.[13] As a new manager, it might look like stopping by every workstation, shaking hands, and listening intently. As a new step-parent, it might mean hearing out the experience of the children, asking the right questions, and validating where they have been.

As the "new guy," there are those who will root for your success and those who cross their fingers hoping for you to fail. Approach with an open heart and learn to affirm and validate those existing teams. It will be a benefit to them and a benefit to you. Why? They will feel more comfortable and assured, which will result in better support and input on all sides.

2. MEASURE YOUR CHANGES

What does a bull in a china shop do? They make unnecessary changes far too quickly, to put it mildly. Be measured and circumspect with the changes you make. Pastor Robert Morris advised me, "Chris, change as little as possible your first year as senior pastor."

There are a few reasons for this. Number one, you need to get comfortable in the position in order to occupy the right head space for big decisions. Two, the fact that you're now the leader is already going to be a difficult change for some to navigate. Don't throw gas on the fire by upending everything that people are accustomed to. This advice is especially true for complete outsiders coming into a company or an organization. In these cases, there is little to no relational capital to start with. Trust must be built over time. When you build trust like this first, people may still question your decisions, but they don't have to question your *motives*. Why? Because you've established the purity of your intentions from the start. Beyond that, a leader needs considerable time to observe, diagnose, and eventually prescribe changes. This observation period might take months or years, depending on the size and complexity of the organization and its issues. Nobody wants a doctor to recommend heart surgery after a quick five-minute checkup. Big changes often require extended observation.

I will give a caveat here and say that some changes obviously need to be made immediately. The "wait a year" advice is a good principle, but not a law etched in stone. For example, I came into my role at the start of the COVID pandemic. Just as I was getting going, we were entering the height of the fear and turmoil surrounding that whole era. Our streaming needed to be ramped up in terms of quality, availability, and processes. I made the decision to throw more resources into that, and I was also required to make decisions about keeping the church open, masks, and so forth. Sometimes big decisions cannot be avoided, even if you are new to the role. The positive is that I had already been at the church for many, many years. This gave me a quicker onramp to being able to make substantial decisions quickly.

3. KNOW THE TRINITY OF PROBLEM-SOLVING

The holy trinity of problem-solving is three key questions: *What needs to stop? What needs to continue? What needs to change?*

With any organization, individual, church, family, or marriage, this triple-threat question must be asked. There are things that need to end. These are the unproductive branches that have to be pruned for the sake of growth. There are other things that should continue. These are the helpful, life-giving, and fruitful aspects that ought to stay in motion. There are other functions that don't necessarily need to be killed off but also shouldn't continue as they are. They just need some tweaking.

As you sift through the aftermath of a major transition, this three-question survey is a great way to identify forward progress. Is the children's ministry falling apart? Ask those three questions. Is your marketing department failing to produce results? Ask those three questions. Is your teenager out of control? Ask those three questions.

If you can identify answers to these three questions, in any given context, you will have begun charting a course to improvement. This "trinity" is a surefire way to build a blueprint for your solution. We could argue that this was the exact model Jesus used when He addressed the churches in the book of Revelation. To the Church of Thyatira, He told them to *stop* tolerating Jezebel (see Revelation 2:24). To the Church of Philadelphia, He told them to *continue* to endure patiently (see Revelation 3:10-11). To the Church of Ephesus, He urged them to *change* their temperature from lukewarm to hot (see Revelation 3:15).

The stop, continue, tweak model will not only give you a course of action but will help keep all pertinent teams accountable to the plan. Having a framework for problem-solving will be crucial, because those under you will have plenty of problems to bring you. This is not a bad thing. In fact, Colin Powell said, "Leadership is solving problems. The day soldiers stop bringing you their problems is the day you have stopped leading them. They have either lost confidence that you can help or concluded you do not care. Either case is a failure of leadership."

4. EMBRACE THE ROCKING CHAIR

After eighty-seven years with no World Series win, the Red Sox were finally in position to take home the trophy in 2004. Tim Wakefield was a rare knuckleballer on the bench and the manager, Terry Francona, was tempted to put him in. He described afterward that when the pitcher on the mound would give up a hit, he would lean forward about to leap up and replace him with Wakefield. When he was throwing well, he would sit back and let him go. He mentioned that he felt like he was in a rocking chair, torn between jumping up and changing things and sitting back to let it play out.

This is the life of a leader. We don't permanently sit on our hands watching the team handle it all themselves. We also don't constantly jump into the mix to micromanage and give input at every turn. We live on the rocking chair—sometimes leaning in and sometimes sitting back. Dennis Mossburg, a leadership consultant based out of Spokane, puts it this way: "Effective leaders learn to strike a balance between micromanaging and laissez-faire managing. Leaders have to be in the Goldilocks zone of leadership: not too much and not too little management."

Be comfortable with the back and forth. If you're uncertain about how you're doing, call in a neutral, third-party observer and get their feedback. Study your team and learn to pick up on their tendencies. Does the room go quiet when you walk in? Are your people desperate for your input and always trying to get a hold of you? Read the clues and lean forward or sit back accordingly.

It's important to approach change with a humble attitude and a willingness to listen to the opinions and perspectives of others. Involve key stakeholders and listen to their concerns and ideas. Building a consensus and a shared vision for the future is crucial in creating buy-in and support for the changes you want to implement.

5. FIND BALANCE

Transition, succession, and the life that comes afterward will require give and take. You might recall seeing old footage of handcars in coal mines. These handcars sat on tracks and the operator would push the lever forward and then pull it back quickly over and over to propel the vehicle down the tracks. As we push and pull in leadership, we are giving forward momentum to our organizations. If we are either *all push* or *all pull*, we go nowhere. This means compromising, conversing, and being willing to pivot. Patience and trust will ease tensions that come along the way.

Having a productive meeting and getting people on the same page can sometimes be like herding cats. It's worth the tension, though. As a leader, it's important to listen in the spirit for what's being said by your team.

Pastor Terry taught me this. You can cut through the chaff by doing this. Often we get distracted from *what* is being said and hung up on *how* people say it. Learn to hear the heart of the Lord while listening to the heart of your people. What words and ideas is God anointing? In this, you won't just be dumping your ideas as the boss but gleaning new ones, too.

The reason this section is called "find balance" is because balance is not automatic. It has to be searched out and pursued. Balanced living does not come by accident. One area that's easy to lose balance in, especially for people in new leadership roles, is what to say *yes* to. When we step into a new position, we naturally want to prove ourselves. You don't want to let any ball drop, and as a result, it's easy to slip into people-pleasing. We run around like corporate soldiers saying *yes* to absolutely everything, working our fingers to the bone with no days off. Everyone wants your time and everyone has an opinion. If you are not careful, you will approve every request and load up your plate with way more than you can handle.

In our case, I inherited an existing elder board. As a result, I had people who saw me grow up in the church for twenty years and now suddenly we were peers. In cases like that, it's very easy to be driven by insecurity to try to perform and prove. Shake off the temptation and let God secure you. Keep your calendar and agenda in sync with the heart of God, nothing more and nothing less. A cluttered calendar won't produce a clear mind. Hear from the heart of God and only approve what He does. Your time is not your own but is on lease from the Lord. Use it in the ways that He desires. Our goal should not be to prove ourselves but to honor the Lord. In doing so, we will prove anything that needs to be proved. Your promotion into a new position is not a license to become a workaholic. Find the balance of diligence and rest and live there. You, your family, your team, and your peers will all be better for it.

PARTING THOUGHTS

Life with God is like being an acrobat on a trapeze. There is always a point of suspension where you let go of one bar and are in mid-air before grabbing the next one. It might be uncomfortable, but you cannot get to the next place until you let go of the first. Oftentimes, God doesn't allow you to see the next door until the first one is shut. If you don't let go, you can't grow.

I'm grateful to have been able to navigate a big transition for my life and career alongside a spiritual father and a group of people who I know have had my best interest in mind. Even with hearts in the right place and everyone on board, even the most prayerful transitions will have shortcomings. There are certainly things we could have done better. For one, more outside counsel would not have hurt. Of course, people spoke into our transition, but it's not a bad thing to bring in many third-party voices. Solomon wrote, "Where there is no counsel, the people fall; but in the multitude of counselors there is safety" (Proverbs 11:14).

Looking back, there could have been more written expectations and clarity over some details. So much of the frustration in any organization is found in the phrase "I thought" or "I assumed." Written expectations cut down on these sorts of statements. While our transition was overwhelmingly positive, there are always little things we will find to improve upon. That's why the *after-action review* mentioned in chapter two is so critical. At the end of the day, as believers, we have good news on our side: You don't fail God's tests. You just take them again.

Whether you are gearing up for a big change or are right in the middle of one, it's never too late to implement the principles of heaven. We know that there is a glorious life waiting for us on the other side of the transition, but what if that glorious life is available in the midst of it, as well?

AFTERWORD

Co-Authored

NOT ALL CHANGE is obvious. A 2005 Merriam article identified several types of transition in life, and one stood out as particularly unique. It's called a sleeper transition.[14] This is a change that occurs gradually without you being aware of the progression. These can be good changes, like if you slowly become more competent with a skill without realizing it. It could also be a bad thing, like the slow collapse of a relationship.

On the other hand, there are nonevent transitions. These are changes that you expect to happen but don't actually unfold. You might be gearing up for good news that never arrives or holding your breath for a promotion that is never offered.

Whether it's a transition that you have planned for like we've described, a sleeper transition that you didn't see happening, or a nonevent transition that never gets off the ground, God has a specific master plan to guide you through.

Any succession or transition can be likened to getting in a car to go on vacation. You could get there in a deluxe vehicle that's comfortable and smooth or you could get there in an old beater, struggling the whole time. Sure, at the end of the day, you got where you needed to go. The transition happened and change occurred. However, the goal is to get there as hassle-free as possible. We hope the timeless principles in this book have helped you to make the journey just a little more smooth.

ABOUT THE AUTHORS

TERRY MOORE is a Founding Pastor and Elder of Sojourn Church. Terry left the business world to begin Sojourn Church in 1987 after a small group meeting in his home grew too large. His passion is to see people set free to experience everything Jesus paid for at the cross. Terry and Susan have been married since 1973, have two adult married children and five grandchildren.

CHRIS MCRAE is the Senior Pastor of Sojourn Church. He joined the Sojourn Staff in 1996 while attending Christ for the Nations. Chris is passionate about impacting the lives of families with the life-changing truth from the word of God. Chris and Vanessa have been married since 1998 and have four children.

ENDNOTES

1. Barna Group. "Leadership Transitions." 2019. Accessed August 2023. https://access.barna.com/wp-content/uploads/2019/08/Leadership-Transitions_Access.pdf.
2. Scientific American. "Our Bodies Replace Billions of Cells Every Day." Scientific American, 23 Feb. 2011, https://www.scientificamerican.com/article/our-bodies-replace-billions-of-cells-every-day/.
3 Graser, Marc (2013-11-12). "Epic Fail: How Blockbuster Could Have Owned Netflix". Variety.com. Variety Media, LLC.
4. Clinton, Bobby, and Haubert, Katherine. The Joshua Portrait: A Study in Leadership Development, Leadership Transition, and Destiny Fulfillment. Barnabas Publishers, 1990.
5. Copenhaver, Martin B. Jesus Is the Question. Abingdon Press, 2014.
6. Munsil, Tracy F. "Shocking Lack of Biblical Worldview Among American Pastors." Arizona Christian University, May 12, 2022. https://tinyurl.com/3aeh8yw4
7. Pennington, Chris. "Why Are People Hard-Wired to Resist Change?" Emerson Human Capital Consulting, https://tinyurl.com/yc43zu72

8. Hartford Institute for Religion Research. 'Fast Facts on U.S. Religion.' Hartford Institute for Religion Research. http://hirr.hartsem.edu/research/fastfacts/fast_facts.html."

9. "Barna Group. 'Why Pastors Are Quitting the Ministry.' Barna Group. Accessed June 5, 2023. https://www.barna.com/research/pastors-quitting-ministry/."

10. McLaren, Samantha. "Internal Mobility." LinkedIn Talent Blog. March 4, 2020. Accessed June 26, 2023. https://www.linkedin.com/business/talent/blog/talent-management/employees-stay-41-percent-longer-at-companies-that-do-this.

11. J Hum Resour. Author manuscript; available in PMC 2014 Apr 29. Published in final edited form as: J Hum Resour. 2010 Summer; 45(3): 718–748.

12. Dimensional Research. "April 2013." Zendesk White Paper: Customer Service and Business Results. http://cdn.zendesk.com/resources/whitepapers/Zendesk_WP_Customer_Service_and_Business_Results.pdf.

13. John Tamming, "Why Are Ministers So Reluctant to Visit Their Congregants?" The Network by the Christian Reformed Church in North America, February 13, 2019, https://network.crcna.org/topic/leadership/pastors/sustaining-pastoral-excellence/why-are-ministers-so-reluctant-visit-their.

14. Transitions in Adult Learning. "Types of Transitions." Accessed 2023. https://transitionsinadultlearning.weebly.com/types-of-transitions.html.

www.ingramcontent.com/pod-product-compliance
Lightning Source LLC
Chambersburg PA
CBHW071717090426
42738CB00009B/1801